GW00724752

THE GOVERNOR'S CAT

A Paperback Original

"To my dear wife Joan,
to whom I gave Solo as a birthday present
shortly before we left for
Gibraltar in 1978."

THE GOVERNOR'S CAT

Sir William Jackson
Governor of Gibraltar, 1978 - 1982

GIBRALTAR BOOKS LTD
Grendon   Gibraltar

First published in Great Britain 1992,
by Gibraltar Books Ltd, Rosehill Farm,
38 Main Road, Grendon, Northampton NN7 1JW

British Library Cataloguing in Publication Data
Jackson, Sir W. G. F.
Governor's Cat
1. Title
636.8

ISBN 0-948466-23-5

© W F G Jackson

All rights reserved. No part of this publication may be reproduced,
stored in a retrieval system, or transmitted in any form
or by any means, electronic, mechanical, photocopying or otherwise,
without the prior permission in writing of the publishers.

Cover designed by Dennis Shearman
using paintings by Vin Mifsud and Lee Nichols

Typeset by Priory Publications, The Priory,
Haywards Heath, West Sussex RH16 4DG
in 11 point New Baskerville on 12 point.
Printed on woodfree paper by FotoDirect Ltd
Unit A2, Enterprise Estate, Crowhurst Road,
Brighton, East Sussex BN1 8AF

CONTENTS

LIST OF ILLUSTRATIONS

PREFACE

This is a true story. All the people in it are real and do exist.
Gibraltar is well worth a visit if you have not been there. The
people are some of the kindest and most generous in the world.
They have every right to be proud of the Rock - their home -
which belongs to them and to no one else.

W.G.F.J.
West Stowell, 1992

CHAPTER 1

JOAN'S BIRTHDAY PRESENT

I first saw Solo sitting in a basket full of American Whites of about her own age. Her blackish brown sooty face and brilliant blue eyes contrasted fetchingly with the total whiteness and yellow eyes of her basket companions. Pick her up? I could not resist doing so!

For a split second, I thought that I had made the biggest mistake of my life. Her first reaction was to swear at me in a most unladylike way. She let out a tiny yet penetrating hiss, curled back her lips showing lots of needle sharp little teeth, stuck all the equally sharp claws of her back paws into my hand, and added insult to injury by bristling out her tail like a sweep's brush.

The mini-hurricane blew itself out almost at once, and Solo displayed one of the strongest facets of her complex personality: an appreciation of her own self interest. As she snuggled down into my arms and began a very small but irresistible purr, I could feel her saying 'He's mine'.

Solo had chosen her Prince Charming. She would soon be leaving all those despicable American Whites behind for good. That would teach them to be so stand-offish and cliquey. And as for calling her an 'Ugly Duckling', she would show them! She had been chosen first, and would soon be whisked off in a crystal coach to the palace of her dreams.

Solo, I should explain, was a princess in her own right, born of two pedigree Siamese: Princess Easter Bunny, her mother, and Prince Kangaroo Chaldean, her father. She *was* Easter Bunny's first litter: she had no brothers or sisters. And as the only kitten of the litter, she was christened Solo, and was soon most dreadfully spoilt. Easter Bunny carried her everywhere with her, showing

1

her off to the other Queens, who had litters of four, five or even six. She would point out how clever she had been to have just one kitten - and a girl too - to whom she could give all her love and attention. Solo was to be brought up properly, and not like some of the other kittens she knew in Mrs Manolsen's cattery.

Mrs Manolsen, in whose establishment Solo was born, decided that this just would not do. Solo would become an impossible person when she grew up, and would never find a decent home, if she was not taught straight away to socialize with kittens of her own age! Unfortunately, there were no other litters of Siamese in the cattery at the time; and so, as soon as Solo was weaned, she was packed off to stay with the family of American Whites where I found her.

Mrs Manolsen paid scant attention to Easter Bunny's protests about *her* Solo being too young to be sent away from home to be schooled with the American Whites. It was time that Prince Kangaroo Chaldean gave her another and, this time, decent-sized litter to pay for the cost of her upkeep. If she could not do better after her next mating, Easter Bunny herself would be looking for another home too!

Moreover, in Mrs Manolsen's view, Solo was indeed an 'Ugly Duckling', and would never become a champion show cat. She had few of the physical characteristics that breeders look for as signs that they have a winner on their hands. Even if Solo did have less obvious psychological assets, like intuition and intelligence, they could not be tested by cat-show judges and so were not to be highly prized. Mrs Manolsen had no qualms about grading Solo as a kitten for a good home, and not for show. She was delighted when she saw Solo's immediate and instinctive choice of me as her salvation, and my obvious attraction to Solo. Good riddance, as far as she was concerned, of an unprofitable kitten. Handing her over to me she said:

"I'm afraid she's no beauty, but I'm glad she is going to a good home."

When I enquired about Solo's price, Mrs Manolsen showed a surprising lack of business acumen.

2

"Oh, you can have her," she said with a hint of relief, "for half my usual fee! I'm sorry she is so plain; but she's all I have to offer at present. You are a bit late in the season for a wider choice."

Few Siamese breeders could have made such a gross error of judgement as this tale will reveal. Personality may be less important than beauty at cat shows, but, in my eyes at least, Solo had both!

I should perhaps explain further why I was looking for a Siamese kitten in the first place. My wife Joan's birthday was in about three weeks' time. We had lost both our thirteen-year-old Siamese, Sooty, and our seventeen-year-old wire-haired dachshund, Strudie, during the four years that we had been living in London while I was Quartermaster General of the Army. I had just retired; our children had left home; and so we felt it was time to start a new animal family now that we were back in the country and settled at last for good after all our travelling in the Service - or so we thought!

Our original animal family - Sooty and Strudie - had joined us in 1960 when we returned from Malaya where I had been Commanding the Queen's Gurkha Engineers. I had been appointed the Colonel, General Staff, in charge of the Minley Manor division of the Army Staff College at Camberley. Our official quarter, Minley Warren, was in an idyllic setting with fields and woods on all sides. There were lots of mice, voles and, I regret to say, birds for Sooty; and rabbits and hares for Strudie. They both lived gorgeous hunting lives there, and continued to do so in all our subsequent postings. But most good things have a habit of coming to an end.

I was lucky enough to be sent up to York as the last Commander-in-Chief of Northern Command, but we and the two animals were only allowed about two years to enjoy the Yorkshire countryside before London closed around us and we found ourselves living in the Quartermaster General's house in Hornton Street in the middle of Kensington. Fields gave way to pavements, and woods turned into the brick and concrete jungles of the metropolis. We and both our animals hated the change.

Sooty was the first to give up. Sadly, she died of cancer while we were away on a tour of the Far East, Australia and New Zealand. Strudie soldiered on for the whole of our four years in Hornton Street. She came down with us to Wiltshire when we were negotiating the purchase of our house for retirement at West Stowell, and realised that paradise was about to return. The lamp posts of Kensington gave way to the real trees and hedgerows of West Stowell. She chased rabbits, dug for voles, and regained the zest for life that had deserted her during her time in London. But regrettably it was all too much for her at the age of seventeen. She overdid trying to recapture her youth. Her back collapsed under the strain, and she did not live to enjoy her old age, savouring the gorgeous country scents.

After this tragedy, I started to scan the local newspapers and shop advertisement boards for suitable replacements. Joan's birthday was in August, which I knew was a bit late for Siamese litters. I had almost given up the quest when I saw a small note stuck in the window of the pet shop in Marlborough, our nearest town, saying 'Siamese kitten for sale: Chaldean cattery'. No telephone number or address was given, but the owner of the pet shop thought that the cattery concerned was in Ogbourne St George. I scanned the telephone directory without success, and so rang the vicar to ask if he knew where the cattery was likely to be. He was very helpful. There was no cattery in Ogbourne, but he had heard of one in Aldbourne, a few miles away.

He was quite right. I drove to Aldbourne, and as I approached the village I saw the sign on the side of the road pointing to the Manolsen establishment. I did not know it at the time, but my quest was over.

Solo's selection of me, and mine of her, was entirely mutual, but there was a snag. There were still three weeks to Joan's birthday. Would Mrs Manolsen, I enquired rather nervously, be prepared to keep her until the actual day so that it could all be a lovely surprise for both Joan and Solo?

"Certainly," replied Mrs Manolsen, "she's a bit young anyway to go off on her own just yet. Three weeks may be a bit long, but never mind, we'll look after her for you."

I was, needless to say, delighted, but here I made a mistake, for which Solo could hardly be expected to forgive me. I put her back into the basket amongst those despicably fluffy and snooty American Whites - the Ugly Sisters in Solo's eyes. The crystal coach had turned back into a pumpkin even before Cinderella could reach the ball; and her Prince Charming had become an unfaithful old toad! Poor little soul, she could think of nothing else to do but to hide in the darkest corner of the basket to cover her shame and disappointment.

I drove back to West Stowell feeling a mixture of elation that I had found a great little companion for Joan and of remorse that I had let Solo down so badly by leaving her behind with the ugly sisters, the American Whites. I stopped the car once and started to turn round to go back to Aldbourne to rescue the little person. Then I remembered Mrs Manolsen' words, 'She's a bit young to be off on her own just yet'; and I knew that I wanted Solo to be a real surprise on Joan's actual birthday. So with a heavy heart I drove off back to West Stowell determined to keep my secret firmly to myself until we could both rescue her in three weeks time.

When I got back Joan was busy with some cooking and so did not ask as she usually did about where I had been. Of course, I had a plausible excuse ready in case she did - something about having one of the tyres on the car seen to in Marlborough - but I did not have to use it. Indeed, I managed to keep my secret intact until her birthday. Then I confessed that I had a very special girl friend whom I wanted her to meet. I was sure, I told her, that she would like her as much as I did! So off we set for Aldbourne.

When we reached Mrs Manolsen's she led us straight down to the shed where I had first met Solo. There she was - my princess - playing with three American Whites, who were, as yet, unsold. I expected her to be ready to spring into my arms and start purring again. Not a bit of it: as I picked her up full of confidence about our mutual affection, she fizzed and spat even harder than she had done at our first meeting, and then dug both her sharp little teeth and even sharper claws into my hands. She had no second thoughts this time; nor did she snuggle down again into my arms and let bygones be bygones. This was the man who had let her down so badly. Not only was she not prepared to give me the benefit of the doubt, but she was also determined to mark me for life. She took a couple of vicious swipes at my face with her soft dark brown, velvet gloved front paws, unsheathing her not-so-soft claws as she did so. She missed, but the fell intention was all too clear.

There was another reason for my discomfiture. During the three weeks since we last met, Solo had ceased to be a loveable bundle of fluff. She was now a gangling teenager - all legs, tail and claws. I handed her quickly to Joan before she could disgrace herself any further, fearing that my surprise birthday present had gone hopelessly wrong, and that I would have to start my quest all over again.

I need not have worried. Solo was no fool. That sense of her own best interests, which I mentioned earlier, came to her's and my rescue. Something told her that she was onto a good thing after all. I might not be worth knowing, but Joan was her very own mistress. She stopped defending herself, and as she settled down in Joan's arms, I could sense her telling the American White, 'I'm not coming back this time. This is my Mistress.'

And so it was that we drove back to West Stowell with the new member of our family. We had brought Sooty's old travelling basket with us in the back of the car, into which we popped her as quickly as possible and shut the wire mesh door, through which we could keep an eye on her during the journey. Sooty used always to scream his head off continuously on any car journey for as long as it lasted, however long it might be. His record had been on our move up to York in 1969, when he managed to scream non-stop all the way! Solo seemed quite stunned by her new situation, and sat quietly looking out of the basket, all eyes for the great outside world that was flashing past the car windows.

She still seemed in a mini-state of shock when we carried the basket into the kitchen to introduce her to her new home. I opened its mesh door and then the fun started! Solo again

6

became a small hurricane of hissing, whirling brown and white fur, and disappeared like lightening into the nearest open cupboard. My doubts about her suitability as Joan's birthday present returned.

CHAPTER 2

THE TAMING OF SOLO

Shakespeare's title, *The Taming Of The Shrew*, is an apt description of our first three days living with Solo. I had misjudged Joan's and Solo's first meeting at Mrs Manolsen's. I thought that Solo's acceptance of her and rejection of me had made them the firmest of friends. The ensuing scene in our kitchen soon showed that their friendship was only fleeting and a matter of convenience as far as Solo was concerned. It was all a question of relativities: Joan was heaven compared to me or the American Whites, but, once outside the security of the cattery, all human beings became mortal enemies to Solo. They had to be watched from various hide-aways and sworn at if they came too near.

The first hiding-place, into which Solo rushed and then chose as a fastness, was a cupboard containing a stack of sized mixing-bowls. As I pushed the door open wide enough to reach in and pull her out, I could just see the tips of her brown ears sticking up over the rim of the top bowl of the stack. In the technical military jargon of tank warfare, she was not just 'hull-down', but completely 'turret-down' as well. Foolishly I tried to put my bare and unprotected hand into the bowl to extricate her, as I intended, gently. It was my hand and not Solo that came out - and far from gently. Those needle sharp teeth had perforated my thumb, drawing a small drop of blood, and the back of my hand was scored with a set of miniature scratch marks, matching the spacing of her claws. First blood to Solo! We decided to leave her to come out on her own when she felt like it.

Three problems arose. What would she eat? Would she use a sand box? We could not let her out into the garden until she had settled down and had agreed to make West Stowell her home.

And where should she sleep?

At Mrs Manolsen's she had been fed on tripe, so Joan, to be motherly, had bought her some on the way home, which smelt the house out as she cooked it for the new member of our family. Mrs Manolsen, who was a vet as well as a breeder of exotic cats, decreed that milk was bad for Siamese. They should only be given water to drink, which should be available to them at all times. So obediently we put down a plate of finely chopped tripe and a saucer of water to tempt Solo out of her lair.

Solo did not emerge from the mixing-bowl cupboard until we had started our supper that evening with grilled trout on the menu, Self-interest - possibly laced with a pang or two of hunger - came to her rescue as usual, and she emerged very quietly to inspect the tripe.

"What do you think I am?" we could almost hear her saying, "An American White, I suppose!"

Her nose whiffled as she savoured the tempting aroma of our trout. That was what she would like and not just common tripe; and she said so in a tiny and very demanding voice. There was that unmistakably, child-like 'I want .....' about what she was saying. So a small dish of trout fragments was set before her.

"That's more like it," she said as she sampled the first mouthful "Siamese Princesses, like me, only eat the best."

From that moment onwards tripe, I am glad to say, as I cannot abide the smell, has never graced her table again! Nor has trout, for that matter. As I will recount later, she does not like oily fish. On her first day at West Stowell, it was again a question of relative values: trout was better than tripe and would do for the time being. What she really liked was non-oily fish like cod or coley. Even salmon was too oily for her fastidious taste.

The sand box problem then arose. Would she know what one was for? As part of my secret preparations for her arrivals I had bought a deepish plastic tray and a bag of the very best cat litter, and had hidden them in the garage. While Solo was enjoying her trout supper, I placed the tray in the corner of the room, not far from where she was eating, on a large sheet of newspaper. When her hunger was satisfied, she stood up, arched her back, shook her back paws in turn, and then sauntered over to the tray.

Shaking her back paws after a meal, we soon discovered, was her way of saying

"I am full, thank you. That was a delicious meal."

Much to our surprise, she hopped into the tray, saying,

"Ah! Good, these people know how to lay things on properly. I do like well organised household arrangements, though I really prefer to go outside to use a flower bed!"

She then gave a very discreet and tidy display of all that Easter Bunny had taught her about cat hygiene. Digging out and filling in was done so neatly that there was not a bit of litter spilled onto the newspaper.

Easter Bunny had clearly been a very good mother in spite of spoiling Solo so dreadfully. As the days went by, Joan often remarked,

"Easter Bunny must have taught Solo so and so. I can't imagine how she knew the rules otherwise."

Digging-out and filling-in were a case in point. Later on when Solo was free to roam wherever she liked, she would select the driest and softest patch in the garden for her sanitary operations. The hole would be dug, tested for size and, if need be, enlarged, reshaped or filled in and restarted until the right fit was achieved. It was clearly an important ritual that Easter Bunny must have spent a great deal of time and patience instilling into her daughter.

Where should Solo sleep? One of my other secret preparations for Solo's arrival had been the purchase of a wicker cat basket as a bed. Inside I placed an old cushion, which looked nice and comfortable, to serve as a mattress. Joan felt that my bed-making was not nearly snug enough for such a small person, so she sacrificed one of her older woollen cardigans to make a warmer nest for that scrap of a kitten.

Providing Solo with a suitably luxurious bed was very important

10

to me personally. I had made a fatal mistake when our previous Siamese, Sooty, had arrived in our family some fifteen years earlier. I had felt sorry for that equally skinny little kitten, and had allowed Joan to take him with her into our bed as a temporary measure while he settled in. He became a permanent lodger whom I never managed to evict. And as he grew larger, so his demands for bed-space increased - at my expense! From the age of one until he died, my allocation was whittled away each night until I was left with little more than a toe-hold by morning.

I was determined that Solo should be allowed no such privileges. It was to be the kitchen for her each night in as comfortable a bed as we could devise, and with a snack bar and sand-box alongside. What more could any reasonable kitten want - even a Siamese? This was to be one of my sticking-points in Solo's upbringing. 'Thus Far' was the family motto on the Jackson coat of arms, and the kitchen was a far as Solo would be allowed to come at night - come wind, weather, snow and ice! Or so I hoped and intended. I did not know Solo very well - as yet!

As bed-time approached on that first evening of Solo's life with us, Joan began to worry. Did I think she would be warm enough? She would hate Solo to be cold as well as lonely now that she was on her own with no other kittens to snuggle up to in the night. Sensing that this was a critical moment for my future comfort as well as Solo's, I stood my ground and a compromise was reached. Solo would stay in the kitchen, but would be given a hot water bottle under Joan's cardigan in her basket.

Fine! But we still had to catch her to put her to bed, and that, on most evenings, was easier said than done. And even when we had succeeded, there was still the problem of getting out of the kitchen quickly enough without the wee person escaping back into the main part of the house. She had an unerring instinct that warned her when she was about to be trapped. Easter Bunny was probably responsible for tuning her instincts so finely. She was certainly well trained in sensing man or woman laid plans for her nightly incarceration in the kitchen. She was as quick as lightning and would always take avoiding action just in time.

Cunning humans that we were, we soon found out that Solo had an Achilles Heel - an overwhelming love of warmth. She just could not resist a warm spot wherever it might be, and however risky exploiting it might be for the maintenance of her personal independence. Later on we could not understand why she would sit for hours on a particular piece of carpet in an otherwise drafty passage. One day I happened to walk across the spot in bare feet. 'Eureka', I had the answer: the carpet was warmed by a central-heating pipe that happened to run underneath the place where she was wont to recline at her ease.

But this knowledge still lay shrouded in the swirling, uncertain mists of the future. On that first night we did not have the advantage of knowing her weakness, but luck was with us. It had been a long, exciting and tiring day for anyone as small as Solo. After eating her trout and digging in her sand-box, she could no longer keep her eyes open however hard she tried. Joan just picked her up and popped her into her basket on top of the warm spot made in the cardigan by the hot water bottle. As we tiptoed out of the kitchen, shutting the door quietly behind us, all that we heard was a small sigh of contentment as she collapsed into a deep sleep.

Solo's second day, facing the terrors of the wide, wild world, was not a success for her or for us. It could be called 'Hunt the Kitten Day'. I arrived downstairs to make the early morning tea, which is one of the menial responsibilities allocated to me in our household routine - I am not trusted with skilled work! I looked in the basket, pulled out the cardigan, and felt under the cushion, but found no kitten. I looked round the kitchen; I inspected all the doors and windows for an escape route, but found no chink through which even the most Houdini-like little person could squeeze; and I vainly called 'puss, puss, puss...' in the most felinely seductive tones that I could muster. Solo had vanished, and was not responding to my frustrated calls of 'Where are you, where are you, you little so and so?'

I was in something of a quandary. I did not want to raise the alarm prematurely, because Joan does not like to be woken too precipitately, and prefers a good half hour in which to drink her tea, watch the early morning news on the T.V. in our bedroom, and decide on her priorities for the day. It would not be very sensible or tactful to tell her as she opened her eyes that her birthday present had somehow escaped from a locked kitchen during the night. After all I had given her a Siamese kitten and not a trained escapologist. On the other hand, if I woke her and could not answer the immediate question, 'How is she?', I would be in deep trouble! I had to do some rapid thinking while the kettle boiled.

My mental agility is never very laudable at such an early hour of the day, but my instincts, like Solo's saved me. I felt that I was being watched, but where from? She could not be watching me from above or below the cupboards because they were the fitted type that ran in one piece from floor to ceiling or up to the draining board and working surfaces. The oven and grill doors were closed, but I looked inside both just to make sure she was not there. All the cupboard doors seemed closed, but I did know that the double doors of the china cupboard did not always latch properly. It was, indeed, ajar so I looked inside, but it was dark and full of stacks of plates, cups, saucers and jugs. The only thing to be done was to start a methodical search operation through the china jungle.

Remembering yesterday's experience with the mixing bowls, I pulled on a pair of rubber kitchen gloves before investigating further. I realised that I might have to shift all the stacks of plates to make sure that she was not using the art of military camouflage to deceive me in my search. She had joined a military household, so she might well be keen to show off all the lessons in field-craft given her by Easter Bunny before she left Mrs Manolsen's.

I started moving the stacks and peering behind them - nothing to be seen. Then I heard a slight clink and an unmistakable hiss that seemed to come from amongst the cups. My direction finding was not very accurate, but I caught a glimpse of a couple of bright little eyes peering at me through a gap between two milk jugs. She was in a perfect defensive position that said much for Easter Bunny's tactical training. Her rear and flanks were covered by the sides of the cupboard's corner, and the jugs gave her frontal protection with a nice observation slit between them. The weakness of her position was that she had left herself no escape route. Using the armoured protection of my gloves, I reached in and pulled out a very un-co-operative, fizzing bundle of fur and was slashed across the cheek for my pains. Second blood to Solo!

The rest of the day went on as badly as it had started. We found that we had to keep all doors and windows shut for our own peace of mind. Even so, peace was an awful long time in coming. We never knew where we would hear that spitting, fizzing hiss coming from next. Joan came down the stairs, carrying the early morning tea tray, and almost dropped it as she drew level with the small ornamental niche half way down, in which various of our military mementos are displayed.

'Fizz, fizz, fizz ....' went something in the niche. At first glance, there was nothing to be seen. Then she saw those tell-tale eyes peering at her from under the ceremonial kukri presented to me when I left the Queens' Gurkha Engineers.

I met my second crisis of the day as I passed the utility room door, and saw the by now familiar figure scamper through it and disappear. The utility room, I realised, was as dangerous as it was attractive to any playful, let alone bellicose, kitten: washing machines, hot air driers, ironers, cupboards full of interesting domestic articles, and piles of washing lying on the floor, waiting their turn for loading, all provided a splendid variety of attractive hiding places. I decided that I must get her out and shut the door on that kitten paradise. Again easier said than done. Joan and I both searched that room high and low without success. She dared not go on with her washing until we were sure that Solo was not in one of the machines.

To cut a long story short, she was, in fact, in the washing machine. At the back there is an exit tube from the fluff extractor, which blows hot air out through a vent in the utility room wall. There should be no gap between tube and the vent, but regrettably when I last cleared the extractor of fluff I had not pushed the machine back properly.

"You don't suppose Solo's got in there do you?" Joan said in desperation.

"Oh no," I replied with totally misplaced confidence, "far too tight a squeeze even for her."

Nevertheless, I pulled the washing machine out from the wall and felt inside the fluff extractor:

"Ouch!" I yelled, as I pulled my hand back and found rather more blood this time dripping from a punctured finger, into which that little varmint had dug her sharp teeth.

"That's third blood to Solo," I said ruefully to Joan as I wrapped my handkerchief round my wounded finger.

While there was now no doubt where Solo was, it would be a difficult tactical problem to get her out. This time she really was in a superb defensive position. The entrance to the extractor was only just wide enough to get my hand in empty, but too narrow to get it out again when holding a swearing bundle of kitten. Once through the restricted entrance, the extractor case widened out into a sizeable cavity, making a nice, comfortable and secure nest for Solo, which she was unlikely to abandon lightly.

"We'll have to leave her to come out on her own." Joan said with a sigh. "She'll emerge when she is really hungry."

She did come out when the smell of our lunch became too much for her. I quickly turned the washing machine back to its original position and pushed it firmly against the wall so that there was no chance of her reoccupying 'Fort Extractor' - the strongest position that she ever managed to find. Her more usual positions were under the easy chairs and beds, in inadvertently open chests of drawers and cupboards, and often in the hollow stems of the pedestal basins in the bedrooms. The essence of her tactics was to hide herself where she could see without being seen. Even the great military engineer, Vauban, would have given her credit for her eye for an impregnable position.

At the end of three days of this nerve-wracking campaign of

kitten warfare, Solo had brought Joan to the point of surrender. She was seriously thinking of ringing Mrs Manolsen, and confessing that Solo had beaten her. I was equally exasperated and would happily have taken her back to Aldbourne straight away. I would not have been averse to donating the fee that I had paid for our tormenter to any charity of Mrs Manolsen's choice in gratitude for the restoration of our peace of mind!

As usual Solo's instincts, together with two bits of luck thrown in, were to be her salvation. The first took the form of Mrs Manolsen's phone being engaged when Joan rang up to pronounce Solo's expulsion. And the second was the showing of James Herriott's *All Creatures Great and Small* on television that evening. I called Joan into the drawing room to watch it, and she momentarily forgot Solo The Terrible. The log fire was burning well as we settled down to watch the behaviour of the Yorkshire vets and the animals and people that they rescued from similar predicaments to ours. Solo could do what she liked now that the decision had been taken to expel her as long as she left us alone until her departure could be arranged.

The programme was just coming to an end and Joan was deeply and emotionally involved with the saga of a stray cat and her kittens being treated by James Farnham, when Solo played her trump card. A small voice reminded us that we were not alone. Then she appeared round the end of the sofa, on which we were sitting, and looked up in a most appealing way that would have softened the heart of even Judge Jefferies.

She came to me first and then had second thoughts. She seemed to say,

"No not you, you've let me down once before."

She turned to Joan and looked up with her bright blue eyes as she had done when I had first seen her amongst the American Whites.

"You'll have me won't you?" she said as she jumped up onto Joan's lap, adding with a sigh as she settled down, "What a day! I've had it."

A small but very audible purr started. There was perhaps one more sigh and she was fast asleep on Joan's lap. She had accepted us and had found her home at last. The war was over. That telephone call to Mrs Manolsen was never made.

CHAPTER 3

WEST STOWELL

Solo could hardly have chosen a better place, in which to grow up, than at West Stowell. It has several areas that are cat heavens. Right outside the old part of the house there is a walled garden with tall wrought iron gates and low lavender hedges along its flagged paths. The brick gate posts are hung with clematis, and the Georgian front of the house carries a very old vine that bears black grapes in summer, attracting all manner of birds ranging from tiny fly-catchers to rapacious jackdaws, which live in some of our disused chimneys. The beds under the walls are filled with roses, shrubs and ground cover of various types to reduce weeding, and provide homes for families of voles and field mice.

The walled garden was paradise to Solo when she was a kitten and can be said to be her first cat heaven. The walls were high enough, and the bars of the wrought iron gates close enough, to shut out any passing dogs, though not other cats. She had security there, whereas the other inhabitants - the birds, small mammals and insects - did not. She was, as yet, too small to catch them, but she had fun trying. And it was just as much fun for us to watch her following Easter Bunny's instructions on what to do, and what not to do, when hunting.

When she arrived at West Stowell it was mid-August and so the lavender was in full bloom, attracting butterflies and bees, which fascinated her. Joan was anxious that she would not know that bees stung. She need not have worried. Solo did remember Easter Bunny's cautionary words:

"Don't touch things that are yellow striped and buzz; they sting!"

We used to watch her from the drawing-room window, sitting by the lavender and cautiously pawing a bee gathering pollen. A small conflict was obviously going on in her mind: the fun of catching something struggled with the memory of her mother's warning. As far as we know, Easter Bunny always won. Solo never came in with a bee or wasp sting, although she ate a number of those horrible blow flies and blue bottles that come over from the cow sheds of the nearby farm.

Solo's second heaven was the outer garden. It was only protected by yew hedges, which, at that time, had not been wired to make them dog-proof. Though not as secure as the walled garden, it had other kitten attractions. In it, there were two large yew trees, a heather bed, catmint bed, a rockery, and, most important of all from Solo's point of view, a bird table - high enough to be out of her reach, but great fun to watch! What could be better? The yews, heather and catmint flowered and seeded at different times of the year and so provided an almost endless stream of birds for Solo to watch and, if possible, catch.

The yew trees were particularly important to Solo because they extend the watching and hunting season well into the winter. The yew berries turn red in the autumn, and draw droves of thrushes, both song and mistle, that come to feast on them. They also bring squirrels, which were the greatest fun to stalk and chase, but were far too alert and wily for a small kitten to tackle. We dreaded the day when Solo would be big enough to take one on. Squirrel bites, like those of rats, usually turn sceptic and can result in nasty ulcers. Sooty, our previous Siamese, had a number of painful visits to the vet for antibiotic injections after being bitten. Solo, however, was to be promoted - though neither she nor we knew it at the time - to higher things before she was old enough to tackle a West Stowell squirrel.

The heather and catmint, like the lavender in the walled garden, gave Solo endless opportunities to exercise her athletic prowess, but regrettably it was the bird table that attracted her attention far more than we would have wished. She may have suffered some doubts about the validity of Easter Bunny's warning on the dangers of catching bees and wasps, but we were faced with an equally difficult conflict of interest: our love of birds clashed with our wish to let Solo enjoy her kittenhood to the full. Fortunately, the bird table was on a four foot high post and so, for the time being at least, was out of her reach. But would she, we asked ourselves, devise some devilish way of trapping our feathered friends? She used to sit contemplating the problem for hours, but no inspiration came to her before we left West Stowell for warmer climes.

Beyond the outer garden lay the vegetable area. The soil of the Vale of Pewsey is very fertile and grows large vegetables of all types in profusion, and, of course, weeds, if you are not persistent with your hoe! Solo was totally uninterested in the size and magnificence of my peas, beans, roots, onions, greens and lettuces, or in the luxuriant weeds. Her delight was in the inhabitants of the vegetable patch and the surrounding hedges: mice, voles, sometimes a baby rabbit or a hedgehog, all living there for her apparent enjoyment.

One thing annoyed Solo in this, her third heaven. Wood pigeons come to devour any un-netted greens. They would strut to and fro with an irritating arrogance, and, when Solo was about, always did so just out of her reach. They were bigger than she was at that time, which was an affront to her in itself, but it was also a challenge. If she could only catch one, she thought, how pleased and proud Easter Bunny would be when she heard about it. It would also show me just how much I underestimated her prowess as a cat Diana! She used to do her best to stalk those 'damned pigeons', as she and I both called them, but catching one remained a dream - for the time being.

Beyond the vegetable garden lies her fourth heaven, and the one that she was to enjoy most when she was fully grown. There are several acres of rough mown grass and woods with a small lake in their midst, which harbour interesting water people like coots and moorhens. Solo liked them because they usually left escape to the very last moment and ran noisily off with a great flapping of wings to the security of the lake. "I might catch one of them", she thought, realising that she had a reasonable chance of perhaps surprising an over adventurous moorhen.

In the evenings, the mallard would land on the lake for their evening meal and to sleep on the island in the middle out of reach of foxes. The rustle of their wings in the twilight, and the splash as they landed, was exciting but catching one was well beyond Solo's ambitions and capabilities. The thought of launching herself out into the water in pursuit of duck never entered her head. In any case, there were more cat-attractive targets around at dusk. Each night, a cock pheasant would meander in from the surrounding fields as it got dark, followed by five or six hens of his harem. They moved quite slowly and sedately, so Solo felt that she had a real chance of a long tail feather, if not a whole pheasant. But when they took off to roost for the night in their favourite trees, they made such a din with their wings and their raucous 'good-night' honking that Solo had second thoughts about them. She would leave pheasants, like pigeon and squirrels, until she was bigger.

After the initial hissing, spitting and generally anti-social phase of Solo's life was over, she began to grow in personality. I have already mentioned her acute sense of her own self-interest. She confirmed this in different ways almost every day. Her choice of knees for a well earned rest was a case in point. Although she loved Joan dearly and did not think much of me, she found my knee bigger and hence more comfortable than Joan's, and so, like a faithless hussy, she would land on my lap and start ingratiating herself with a rumbling purr.

She was most likely to select my knee, I noticed, whenever I was wearing a dark suit that would show every one of those small white hairs that she was apt to leave behind when her rest was over. I would not have minded if I had still been a serving general with a batman to look after my clothes, but I was retired and had to do all the brushing down myself. Solo never gave any thought to my feelings, but I observed that she would leap onto the knee of any guest wearing a dark suit. It was as if Easter Bunny had given her a short lesson in physics, stressing the heat absorbent properties of various suiting materials.

"Take my advice", she must have said, "always go for the dark suited ones. They're the warmest and cosiest!"

She also had that contrary habit of most cats of leaping onto the lap of the guest who least likes them. It seemed as if she felt that she must show that Siamese are different from ordinary cats and should be loved by everyone. She usually got away with it except on one famous occasion that I will recount later.

I have also mentioned her inbred tactical instincts that made her so difficult to find and capture during her first few days at West Stowell. But I was never able to fathom the reasoning behind her definition of a straight line. It was certainly not the shortest distance between two points. Her view was that to get from A to B you should zigzag your way there, giving each piece of furniture an affectionate rub on the way.

Straight lines were anathema to Solo, which I could understand in the garden or woods where keeping to cover made good tactical sense, but why keep to cover in the safety of the house? To give her maximum credit, she could be said to be the mistress of the indirect approach, except that I doubt if she ever knew where she would end up when she started one of her zig, rub, zag, rub, zig... movements across any part of the house.

This quirk of indirectness manifested itself in other ways. She could never bring herself to allow anyone, however well meaning, to pick her up at first attempt. As you bent down, she would side-step and dart a few paces away from you, clearly muttering to herself, 'Missed!', under her breath; then 'Missed again!' as you lunged a second time. When she had made whatever point she had in mind, she would roll over on her side, saying 'You can pick me up now if you like, but stroke my back first.'

All would be well, particularly if you did as you were asked and stroked her back. Woe betide you if you dared to tickle her tummy. It brought out, literally, all her worst features - hiss, teeth, claws and vicious kicks with her back legs as she tried, often successfully, to rip your hand. It was always far less painful to pander to her whims, and to avoid her tummy. If you were polite and stroked her back, she would stretch out purring as if to say 'More, more, more...'.

Besides objecting to having her tummy touched, she had two

Above: Plate 2. West Stowell.   Below: Plate 3. West Stowell's lake

West Stowell 1991. Above: Plate 4. Solo, the Governor's cat (retired).
Below: Plate 5. Heidi and Trudie, Solo's friends. (Photo Stuart Hamilton-Towler)

other important, but negative, characteristics: obstinacy and inquisitiveness. Both were to lead us and her into all sorts of trouble over the years. A Siamese princess, like Solo, must be allowed to decide everything for herself. Apart from Easter Bunny, I doubt if she ever listened to or took advice from anyone. Put her down in the warmest and apparently most comfortable chair in the house, and she would invariably jump off at once, indicating that she would be the sole judge of where she would sit. If she had not been christened Solo very appropriately by Mrs Manolsen, I am sure we would have called her Mary after 'Mary, Mary, quite contrary...' of the nursery rhyme.

Her inquisitiveness or curiosity - the proverbial cat killer - was much more dangerous. She could never resist a half open cupboard or drawer; or, indeed, any door that was not firmly shut. She would get into anything that she could prize open with her soft but remarkably strong and flexible paws. The contents just had to be inspected. Sometimes she would jump into a drawer whilst your back was turned, and be completely hidden when you came to shut it: result, lost kitten, and searches high and low for her! As one of the doors into the garden was open more often than not, there was no way of telling whether she was in the house or not until a plaintive, high pitched yell would eventually be heard coming from inside some piece of furniture!

Solo loved my desk. It gave her inquisitiveness full rein. Or perhaps she felt that I was the untidiest person she had ever met. Whatever the reason, she was sure that she must sort things out for me each morning while I was working at it. This was, of course, in the days before I had invested in a word-processor. I used to write my books with soft 2B pencils, good paper and an efficient eraser, always claiming, until I learnt better, that they were as good and far cheaper than any computer available in the mid-1970s. My system meant that my desk was littered with pencil ends, pieces of eraser and rolled up balls of discarded drafts, as well as all the usual bric-à-brac on an author's desk. It really was a challenge to a tidy-minded kitten.

Solo's method of sorting out my desk was simplicity itself. In her view, it should have a clear working surface, unencumbered in any way. Using her sharp little teeth, she delighted in removing the pencil stubs from their jar, and then rolling them gently across the desk with her soft dark brown paws until they fell onto the floor. The erasers would follow, but the greatest fun of all was knocking down the paper balls and following them herself to toss and scatter them playfully around my study. Little did I realise it at the time, but she was having a bit of preliminary mouse-baiting practice, which her instincts, or Easter Bunny, had told her would become her first love in the days to come.

It was not long before the first mouse did arrive. We had decided that Solo was sufficiently settled at West Stowell to enable us to stop buying expensive cat litter, and to let her to go out at night to do her digging. We installed a cat flap in the back door, and I gave her cat flap training, which she resented. Princesses expected doors to be opened for them: she was not going to scramble in such an undignified way through that ghastly device, which caught her tail anyway as she pulled herself through it. Nevertheless, when she thought we were not looking, we would hear the 'Clonk, Clonk' of the flap as she slithered through it surreptitiously into the freedom of the garden. It became her secret passage, which we were supposed to know nothing about. She never used it in our presence, sitting instead at the door and looking up at the handle, asking to go out the easier and more dignified way.

On 'First Mouse' Day, we heard the tell-tale 'Clonk, Clonk', which seemed a bit louder than usual, suggesting greater haste and possibly excitement. Solo rushed into the drawing-room where Joan was sitting on the sofa doing some sewing. She gave an unmistakable growl, a thing that she had never done before to our knowledge. Apart from her obvious excitement, there seemed nothing else unusual about her sudden rush into the house. Then she opened her mouth and Joan screamed. She had dropped a bemused, but very live little shrew onto the carpet, and then started a war dance around it.

"Look what I've got; look what I've got!" she seemed to be chanting; "Aren't I clever; aren't I clever!"

I tried to grab her, but she was too quick. Pouncing on the shrew, she had it back in her mouth and dashed off into the study. Then evading another of my desperate, but clumsy lunges, she was off upstairs to our bedroom with her prize. She was furious with me for failing to congratulate her on her prowess, and for not allowing her to show off her skills in emulating one of Spain's most experienced matadors.

What shrews in general lacked in size and ferocity compared with bulls, they certainly made up for with speed and agility, so Solo considered shrew-baiting as fair a sport as bullfighting. On this particular occasion, she had only one thought in mind: how to stop me robbing her of her prize. She added 'Shrew-snatching' to my list of delinquencies.

It must have taken me half an hour to rescue that shrew. Each time that I was near success, Solo managed to sweep it up in her mouth and disappear under the bed, wardrobe or dressing table. I tried to concentrate on catching the shrew every time she let it run. This was clearly poor anti-kitten tactics: Solo always beat me to the snatch! It dawned on me slowly that I should change my methods and mount a two phase operation: first, I should catch Solo and then, in the second phase, I should go to the rescue of her captive. Initially, the first phase was just as unsuccessful, but then I was lucky enough to catch her by the tail. This was an excellent hold as it forced her to drop the shrew in order to yell at me. The shrew fell out of her mouth and scuttled for cover.

The second phase, on this occasion, was quite quick and simple. The shrew was as exhausted as I was and made no attempt to escape when I found it nestled down in a corner of the room between the carpet and the skirting board. Gently lifting it up in my handkerchief, I took it into the walled garden and let it make its final escape.

I was not so lucky in subsequent shrew hunts. The technique of catching Solo by the tail was infallible, but finding the jettisoned shrew afterwards was much more difficult. The quicker I caught Solo, the more life was left in the shrew and the greater was its ingenuity in evading re-capture. There must be several mummified shrew corpses underneath the fitted cupboards in the kitchen. The shrews could squeeze into one or two of the less well fitted places, and we could not extricate them without pulling the kitchen to pieces. Faced with the choice of a second joust with Solo or starvation, they seemed to choose the latter as we rarely saw them again - or smelt them for that matter. They just disappeared.

One shrew led a particularly charmed life. Solo brought it in and I quickly caught her by the tail. The shrew, as usual, fell out of her mouth and disappeared. I looked high and low for that shrew without success. Next day I noticed Solo sitting patiently by a curtain in the drawing-room. She was certain that there was something interesting in that curtain. I shook it, but nothing fell out, and I told her that she was mistaken. Joan noticed the same thing later that afternoon when the sun was low and streaming into the room. She, too, shook the curtain without reward, but was more inquisitive than I had been. She held out the curtain, which was made translucent by the sun, and gave a scream. I rushed in from the study to see what all the fuss was about:

"Quick, there's a mouse in the curtain!" she cried, "Do something!"

Sure enough, when I held out the curtain, I could see the silhouette of a tiny person, scrambling further up for safety. The shrew was in between the main curtain and the lining, which was not stitched at the bottom so that it could hang loose, and had provided sanctuary. Joan swept up Solo, who was muttering something that sounded uncommonly like 'I told you so', and locked her in the study while I coaxed the shrew out of the curtain. It was sensible enough to let me catch it and return it to the garden to fight another day - and, of course, to breed more of its kind for Solo's entertainment and Joan's disquiet.

Shrews soon gave way to voles, and voles to larger and fatter mice in Solo's gladiatorial calendar. There must be a difference in the cat-appetising smell of shrews and voles on the one hand and mice on the other. Solo never thought of eating the former, but had a craving for the latter. Nevertheless, her first mouse was a disaster.

We were out when she caught it, so we did not see her rush up to what was to become her favourite mouse parlour - our bedroom. There she carried out her first experiments in mouse dissection, and ate the centre portion, leaving the head and tail for afters. On this occasion there were to be no afters: she was violently sick on our clean bedspread, and I had to clean up the mess and her afters. The stain has never really come out, despite several journeys to the dry cleaners. As for Solo, she was not put off eating mouse, nor from using our bedroom for her cat-gourmet feasts, if she could get away with it.

The days were coming when we had to decide whether Solo should remain a 'She', or become an 'It'. Down to the vet she went for her first medical examination. We had always had trouble with our old Sooty in cars. He would yell his head off continuously however long or short the journey might be. His record was continuous vocal complaint from London to York when I took over Northern Command in 1969. Solo proved to be no better as far as cars were concerned. She sang, 'I don't want to go! I don't want to go!' all the way down to the vet's surgery.

When we got there, she took to Mr Ward at once and appointed him her doctor. She confided in him that we had been exceptionally cruel to her, loading her into that terrible travelling cat-basket for her long journey to visit him. She ignored my protest that the trip had taken less than ten minutes. And Derek Ward became her patron saint when he decided, much to her delight, that she was still too small to be operated on. He suggested coming back after Christmas. She was not likely to become attractive to Toms until about Easter time.

As Christmas approached, mousing became less compelling. It was too wet and cold outside for it to be much fun. We put her night basket, equipped with a soft cushion and one of Joan's cast-off woolly cardigans, under a radiator as her winter quarters, which she thought was very civil of us. Indeed, she liked it so much that she spent most of the winter months in it, and so was always easy to find.

When the snow came just before Christmas, Solo thought it the greatest fun. She would jump through it like a small kangaroo and did not seem to mind the cold on her paws and tummy. Her white and brown fur gave her excellent camouflage in the snow, and for a time she resumed her hunting programme with birds as her quarry. This did not last long. The blackbirds, who, until then, had not paid much attention to her, began to recognize her as a threat. Food on the bird table had become more important to them, and so they mobbed her every time she appeared near it. They would dive at her, making that high pitched, angry blackbird squawking noise, which terrified her.

The combination of blackbird blasphemy, cold paws and tummy, and failure to achieve anything worthwhile brought Solo's short winter hunting season to a close. Her energies were henceforth devoted to indoor sports. I had bought our Christmas tree in the Marlborough market, and had stood it in a sand filled bucket in a corner of the drawing room ready for decoration. As usual I could not remember where I had stowed the Christmas decorations when I packed them away the year before. I found them eventually in totally different boxes from the ones for which I had been looking. I had forgotten that for our move from London, I had repacked them in new boxes, and had thrown the old, venerable, but tattered ones away.

Solo had the time of her life helping me decorate the tree. The multi-coloured glass balls were every bit as attractive as mice and birds, especially the ones that tinkled as she pawed them. The tinsel provided delights as she wrapped herself up in it, and then tried to un-wrap herself by rolling onto her back and kicking vigorously with her back paws. I had to rescue her several times before she could strangle herself.

The apple of her eye was the little angel, which always adorned the top of our tree. She pawed her lovingly with an acquisitive glint in her eyes as I climbed onto a chair to fix her in position. Solo gave me a disapproving look, which I returned with malevolent over-confidence, as I took the angel away from her. The bottom of the tree was, I thought, high enough off the ground to stop her leaping onto a lower branch and shinning up the stem to rescue the little angel from her precarious perch.

All went well for a couple of days. Then Joan noticed a few bit of tinsel on the floor under the tree. I said that they must have slipped off; it was my fault for not fixing them properly. Next we found a couple of the coloured glass balls smashed on the floor. I took responsibility again for bad workmanship, and suggested that the wind had blown them off. Joan was less charitable and accused Solo of sabotage, but I defended my helper with a misplaced loyalty, which Solo did not reciprocate.

Next day we went into Marlborough to do our last shopping before Christmas. When we got back, we found the drawing-room in chaos. The tree was on the floor; the decorations were strewn around the room; and Solo was sitting on the sofa with the little angel held endearingly between her paws. She looked at us as if to say:

"It wasn't me. He didn't put it up properly. The wind blew it over. I've done my best to sort out the decorations for him."

Joan was not amused; nor, for that matter, was I. Solo and I spent the afternoon making good the damage. This time I used a bigger, deeper bucket with lots more sand, and removed some of the lower branches. Neither the wind nor Solo were to be able to rescue the little angel from the top of the tree again.

Solo and I got to understand each other better over the Christmas tree incident. We had both been at fault, and we had the common bond of having incurred Joan's displeasure. The temperature outside was down to freezing, and I knew that the kitchen where Solo slept must be very cold at night when the central heating went off. Solo did not complain about being put to bed there, but my new found loyalty to her pricked my conscience. It was to be my undoing.

I suggested to Joan that Solo should be allowed to sleep in the drawing-room as long as the cold lasted. Joan pointed out quite rightly that, if I wanted to go on putting back the Christmas tree decorations each morning, it was a splendid idea. Why not be sensible and let her share our bedroom as Sooty used to do? We could keep an eye on her there, and make sure that she did not get cold. I was caught on the proverbial Morton's fork! If I agreed to Solo sharing our bedroom, it would not be long before I would be back to my nine inch bed ration: but, if I stuck to my earlier principle of no Solo in the bedroom and she stayed in the kitchen in severe winter weather, I would lose her new found loyalty, if not love, for me! I was weak minded and chose the latter. I told Solo quite firmly that she could sleep in our room for as long as the freeze lasted, and then she must to go back to the kitchen. Solo agreed, but has slept in our bed ever since!

With the turn of the year Derek Ward's estimate of when Solo would first become attractive to Toms went awry. She should have come into season in April, but the tell-tale signs appeared in January. We decided to rush her down to her doctor straight away. Derek Ward could not be as co-operative as he would like to have been; nothing could be done until her period was over. Little did we know what that meant. I would never knowingly wish the next week on even my worst enemy. It was horrific!

On Derek Ward's advice, we confined Solo to the house, and provided her with a sand box again - a thing that she thought that she had outgrown for ever. I closed the cat-flap by sticking a piece of cardboard over it with Sellotape, and we made sure all the windows on the ground floor were kept shut. We also reminded ourselves and Heather, who cleaned for us, that we must never open an outside door without making sure first that Solo could not follow any of us out into the garden where some amorous Tom might be waiting in hiding for his opportunity.

On the second day of Solo's confinement, we had a taste of things to come. Solo started patrolling up and down, letting out pathetic moans about how unreasonable we were being. If we would let her out, she would promise to come back straight away after she had completed her daily hygiene. She would even forego her round of the gardens to maintain discipline amongst the mice, voles and smaller birds, if we would just let her out for a short time. I don't think she was fibbing, because I doubt if she knew that what she really wanted was a Tom.

As the day wore on the moans turned to wailing, and then to

louder and louder howls. I began to realise why there are so many half-Siamese cats about. It takes great courage and determination to keep a young Siamese princess incarcerated when she wants to start a family. It also needs not only willpower, but wits as well, as we were soon to find out.

It was not long before Solo started to tear at the cardboard stuck over her cat-flap. I decided to thwart her by placing our large Moroccan pouffe against it. It was many times heavier than she was, so I felt reasonably confident that there was no escape for her that way. By the grace of God, I caught sight of her pushing herself in between the pouffe and the door. The pouffe was not heavy enough to stop that powerful love-lorn kitten, and would soon have been pushed clear of the cat-flap, if I had not intervened. It would not have taken her long to tear off my flimsy cardboard cover if she could have reached the cat flap, which I was determined she should not.

I looked around for something heavier and remembered that I had a five-gallon plastic water container in the garage. I filled it about half full so that it was not too heavy for me to lift, and replaced the pouffe with it, saying 'move that you mini-Hercules!' She did. I had forgotten that it was not a question of lifting the container, which was at least ten times her weight, but of levering it aside on Heather's highly polished kitchen floor. Again we were lucky enough to catch her in the act.

The solution was ready to hand. I filled the container to the brim and pushed it back against the cat-flap. I could barely lift it and even sliding it was not easy. Try as she would, Solo could not shift it - Round 1 to me!

There are always two or three sides in any battle of wits. In this case, it was not just me and Solo involved, but her potential suitors as well. How they did it, I do not know. Solo had never left the house since our abortive visit to the vet, and yet Toms started roaming around the house in growing numbers. There are several farms nearby, each with its belligerent rat-catcher Tom. They came in all shapes, sizes and colours, each showing off his battle-scared ears to convince Solo that he was worthy of her hand.

She, for her part, sat in the window, preening herself like any professional in a red light district and egging them on.

At first she just looked demure and fluttered her long eye lashes. Then she spied a long haired tabby with cauliflower ears, who took her fancy. She obviously thought him gorgeous - just her type, she seemed to think. She let forth a horrendous Siamese mating call, and a deafening catterwalling started as she tried to tell him through the glass of the drawing-room windows that she loved him. I rolled up a newspaper and went to the door intending to frighten him away, making a cracking noise by slapping it hard against a wall. Solo was down from her window in a flash, ready to accompany me. Joan grabbed her just in time to stop her, and was severely scratched for her pains. Round 2 was a draw: Solo did not got out, but she had drawn blood - Joan's!

The third round lasted for the whole of the next three days. As far as the Toms were concerned, Solo sang with all the beguiling charm of the Lorelei on the rock in the Rhine: to us it was like the agonised shrieks of a wounded hyena - or what we thought a wounded hyena would sound like. It was a continuous round-the-clock performance, which was very wearing for us, but she herself never seemed to tire. Although we never gave in, and thwarted every move in this ear pounding boy-meets-girl saga, we were nervous wrecks by the end of it. We did win this third and last round, but only narrowly on points!

Solo's passion subsided as quickly as it had begun. She stopped shrieking at the Toms and moaning about how unfair I was being. The Toms disappeared almost as miraculously, their frustrated ardour quenched. The five gallon container was lugged away from the cat-flap, and the denizens of the garden scuttled for cover as Solo resumed her patrols, the enforced armistice between them and Solo being at an end. A few days later she was in her cat basket again, and on her way down to Derek Ward for her operation. She received little sympathy from us. 'Never again', Joan and I said in unison as we reached the vet's surgery.

Derek Ward asked us to collect her that evening. He warned

us that she would be a bit dopey from the anaesthetic. She would have a couple of stitches in her side, but she should recover very quickly, provided we kept her quiet for twenty-four hours. He would take her stitches out if we would bring her back to him in a week's time.

None of this happened. When I collected her at about five o'clock, she was far from dopey. She told me with a loud purr that she was delighted to see me again. Her accent wasn't even slurred when she miaowed as I picked her up. Her gait was steady and unaffected by the two stitches I could see in a bald patch on her side. Back at West Stowell, she tucked into a hearty meal of her favourite non-oily fish, and settled down on our bed to sleep it off.

When it was time to take Solo back to Derek Ward to have her stitches out, we discovered she had done the job herself. I had brought the hated cat basket down, when Joan exclaimed in surprise 'They're gone!' Solo had gradually licked them undone and they had vanished.

The scar on her side took a great deal longer to disappear. When she had arrived back from her operation, there had been a largish patch of pink bare skin where the fur had been shaved off around the incision. As the hair grew again, the patch turned black and stayed that way for several weeks. No white hairs appeared, and Joan became quite fussed: were we to have a Siamese with a black patch on her side for life? I tried to restore her confidence in Derek Ward by saying that all Siamese fur started out black, though I had no experience or reason for saying so.

It took about six weeks for my supposition to be proved correct. Very gradually the black patch disappeared and Solo was her beautiful self again, and that terrible week of siege warfare with the farmyard Toms became no more than an unpleasant memory.

CHAPTER 4

GOVERNOR'S CAT (DESIGNATE)

I had been retired from the Army about six months when a crisp blue envelope with the royal coat of arms on the back tumbled through the letter-box one morning. It was from the Permanent Under-Secretary of State at the Foreign and Commonwealth Office. He said that on the advice of the Foreign Secretary, the Prime Minister wished to advise Her Majesty, the Queen, that I should be appointed Governor of Gibraltar in May 1978. Would I let him know whether I would be prepared to accept the appointment?

I would have been delighted to do so without any hesitation, but I was not sure what Joan would say. She had 'followed the drum' with me for more than thirty years in our innumerable postings around the world, and I knew she wanted to settle down and enjoy our retirement. West Stowell was our first real home, and the paint was barely dry on the redecoration. And, of course, there was Solo to consider!

When I showed Joan the letter, she looked wistfully out of the window at the walled garden and our peaceful surroundings, obviously comparing them with her vision of the Rock. We had visited Gibraltar on a number of occasions quite recently, but we had never served there. She knew that the Spanish political and economic siege, that had been going on since the Queen's post-coronation visit in 1954, had not ended as many people had hoped and expected when Franco died in 1975. With the frontier still closed, living there was bound to be claustrophobic, or so we both thought at the time, though we were to be proved wrong later.

But there would be the compensations of the warm Mediterranean climate, and being only about two hours' flight away from our son and daughter in England. Nigel was a captain in the Green Jackets, and Rosie had recently married a Sapper like myself, Captain Reid, who had been one of my A.D.C.s in York. Joan did not want to be too far away, if and when they started a family. Moreover, we could always come back to West Stowell when we were on leave.

Wistful though Joan's look may have been, she knew that what I really wanted was a new challenge in life. I was not ready to retire, although I had passed the Army's retiring age of sixty for full generals. Indeed, she had been worrying about how I would manage to wind down after a very active and, at times, exciting life. For the first few months of my retirement, there had been plenty to do sorting out West Stowell, but she knew that this would not last, or be enough to stop me getting 'itchy feet'!

She did not take long to reach her decision. Picking Solo up from the sofa where she had been curled up fast asleep, she said,

"Of course, you must accept, but I'll only come with you, if Solo can come too!"

The deal was clinched then and there, and I posted my letter of acceptance. And so it was that Solo became the Governor's Cat (Designate), and I started to think out how I would try to help the Gibraltarians to win the 15th Siege of the Rock.

When we told Solo that she would be going out to Gibraltar as the Governor's cat in about four months' time, she seemed suitably impressed, but then realised that she too would be saying a painful farewell to West Stowell, and to her mice and bird friends there, though they would be delighted to see the back of her. We did not tell her that the price of a sojourn in the warm Mediterranean would be six months quarantine on her return to England. That was looking far too far into the future for someone as young as Solo to worry about.

While I started planning what we should take out, and what should be left behind, and while Joan was working out what clothes she would need, Solo decided that she must train herself to be the Governor's Cat. Quite what she envisaged the duties of the Governor's Cat to be is her secret, but she seemed to assume almost straight away the mice and small birds were now beneath her dignity as quarry. She set her mind on bigger prey: possibly a rabbit or pheasant would prove her suitability for her future role. She might be able to catch one, she thought, now that she was a little bigger. She was determined to prove herself to me by fair means, or perhaps, as it turned out, by foul!

Rabbits were unfortunately hard to come by: myxomatosis had killed off most of them around West Stowell some years ago, and the farmers made certain that there was no recovery of the rabbit population around us. Hares were a possibility, but a bit too big for a year-old kitten, even though she was to be called to higher things. A pheasant would be ideal, but a bit too big as well. But what about a wood pigeon? Could she catch one feeding on my vegetables? That would certainly kill two birds with one stone. She would earn my gratitude for protecting my greens, while at the same time proving herself for her new elevated status.

One of the tasks that I had to complete before we left for Gibraltar was to dig and set the vegetable garden for the year so that our daughter, Rosie, and her husband could benefit from the fertile soil of West Stowell. They were living quite close at Barton Stacey near Andover, and offered to look after our house while we were away. While I was digging diligently one afternoon, I heard a great flapping of wings on the far side of the hedge as a number of pigeons took off. Looking through a gap in the hedge, I saw a very frustrated Solo still in a crouch, looking up at her departing targets.

A couple of days later, I was in the kitchen making the early morning cup of tea, which I was about to take up to Joan in our bedroom. The cat flap went 'Clonk, Clonk' behind me, and Solo darted through the kitchen and off up the stairs. She was so quick and obviously excited that I knew that she had caught something, which she was intent on carrying up to Joan as a good-morning present. Perhaps she might be trying to show that it was not only early birds that catch worms. Joan might like to get up a bit earlier and follow her example. It was quite the best time of the day for hunting!

Leaving the tea tray in the kitchen, I rushed up the stairs in an attempt to intercept Solo before she could deposit a mangled corpse on our bed. Fortunately, the bedroom door was shut and I managed to collar her before she could reach the guest bedroom, which she was apt to use as an alternative dissecting room if she could not get to her favourite spot behind Joan's dressing-table. Out of her mouth fell not a mouse or shrew but a small wad of bluish-grey feathers.

"Damn you! You beastly cat." I said, shaking her rudely by the scruff of her neck. "You've killed one of our favourite blue tits."

Joan was as upset as I was, but there was nothing we could do about it. Cats catching birds was all part of the balance of nature, and certainly in Solo's view she should have been praised rather than scolded for her efforts. On this occasion she was right, although I did not know it at the time, but was soon to find out.

On the way back to the kitchen to recover the tea-tray, I picked up one or two more feathers that must have belonged to my supposedly departed blue tit friend, feeling miserable about the whole episode and very displeased with Solo. "Why couldn't she take on something more her own size?" I muttered to myself on my way down the stairs.

In the kitchen, I saw some more feathers on the back door mat, and, on looking closer, I saw that the cat flap was splattered with blood. What had been going on? Had there been a cat fight? Or had some intruder tried to come through the cat flap and been repelled by Solo? I had seen no blood on her, but I had not been expecting to do so and had not inspected her. I would do so when I got back to the bedroom with the tea.

Then I remembered that I had not collected the newspapers and milk off the back door step, so I unlocked and opened the door. There were the papers, all splattered with blood, and beside the milk bottle lay the corpse of a wood-pigeon - dead but still warm.

How Solo had caught it, we will never know. Later I found a mass of feathers in the kitchen garden where a great battle had taken place. But equally mystifying was how that small kitten had managed to drag her prize over the two hundred or so yards back to the house when it was about twice her size. The blood on the back-door step showed that she had struggled to bring the corpse through the cat flap, but that had proved just too much for her. The mouthful of blue feathers that she did bring in were from the pigeon's neck, and were a token to show us how well she was getting on with her training for her future role.

Solo was, quite naturally, very proud of her feat of arms. In her eyes, and in ours too, she had won her spurs as the Governor's Cat (Designate). She felt that she must now consolidate her position. Fortune certainly seemed to be smiling on her and favouring the brave. A few days later when we returned from shopping in Marlborough, we found another dead pigeon lying right in the middle of the kitchen floor. She must have managed the extraordinary feat of dragging or pushing the corpse through the cat flap. She was patrolling up and down the kitchen, rubbing herself against the cupboard corners and proclaiming:

"Look what I've done; just look what I've done."

I regret to say I fell for the whole artful performance - hook, line and sinker! I picked her up and congratulated her, saying that I would take everything back that I had said about her catching blue tits. Certainly she had won her spurs for a second time. It would be an honour to take her to Gibraltar with us. It never crossed my mind to wonder how it was that there was no blood splattered about this time.

Joan has often accused me of jumping to unwarranted conclusions, and regrettably she is more often proved right than I am ever prepared to admit. When I put Solo down, she went back to holding vigil over her second pigeon victim, lying in state, feet up and claws curled, on the kitchen floor. 'Lying' was the correct description of the pigeon's state: 'Liar' was the word that I should have applied to Solo far quicker than I did, had I not fallen for her feminine feline guile.

I took an old newspaper and carried the corpse out to the dustbin, and thought no more about Solo's extraordinary agility until I met Nick Dover, one of our neighbours, later that day. I told him that we were blessed with an efficient pigeon exterminator, who was very proud, as we were, of her feats of valour. He looked suitably impressed as I told him the story, but then queried the validity of Solo's second claim. He had found a very sick pigeon in his garden and had put it out of its misery.

"I put it under the yew hedge of your outer garden, intending to remove it later, but I forgot," he explained, "let's see if it is still there."

Sure enough, when we reached the spot, Nick's suspicions were confirmed: the pigeon corpse had gone!

" The little fibber!" I exclaimed, "I didn't feel her second pigeon, but now I come to think of it, the way its feet were curled up did suggest that rigor mortis had set in..."

How Solo caught her first pigeon has remained a mystery. It was certainly warm when I picked it up. Her second catch was a monstrous fib. Her only feat was dragging it so far, and hauling it through the cat flap. However, to this day, she is not aware that I know she told a whopping lie to consolidate her claim for promotion to Governor's Cat (Designate).

Being a cat of such distinction had disadvantages, as we were about to find out. I consulted Derek Ward, the vet, about inoculations, export licenses, import licenses, and so forth to make sure that there would be no last minute hitches in Solo's despatch to Gibraltar when the time came for us to leave West Stowell. The inoculations were simple enough: Derek promised to give her the right ones, the right number of days before her departure. Export permits, he said, were, in his experience, a bit more tricky. Applications had to be made to the Ministry of Agriculture and Fisheries on a special form that could only be supplied by the Ministry itself.

I wrote off to the Ministry, using all the best and most convoluted Civil Service jargon that I had acquired over some fifteen years' service, on and off, in the jungles of Whitehall in various military appointments. The forms did arrive after a suitably long pause, designed, I felt sure, to demonstrate that the mandarins were totally unimpressed with Solo's future status, and that the Ministry was too understaffed and underpaid to clear its backlog of applications any quicker, even for a Governor's Cat.

As soon as I started to read the application form, my heart sank. No export license would be considered without the presentation of an import license from the country of destination. Moreover, the actual application form must be submitted not more than three weeks before the intended date of departure, and not less than a fortnight before it! The eye of the bureaucratic needle was thus only one week wide. A postal strike or some other act of God could send all our best laid plans awry.

I had started my quest for a license early enough to cope with Whitehall's usual sluggishness, but I had underestimated the effects of the southern European climate on the speed of reaction of the Gibraltar Government, whose bureaucracy is modelled on the British system, but is slowed by 'Mañana'. My application for an import license went off, and the days went rapidly by without any noticeable reaction from Gibraltar. I must admit that I had assumed that an application from their new Governor would have speeded up their normal response time. In the end, I rang up my future personal staff to enquire whether my application had been received in the Government Secretariat?

Commander Tom Le Marchand, Royal Navy, who was to be my Military Assistant and had gone out three months earlier to run in my new team before I arrived, did some quick research and rang me back. Yes, the application had arrived, but regrettably the official, who received it, was blissfully unaware that there was to be a change of Governor and did not know who I was anyway! His only plea in mitigation was that I had not marked my application 'Urgent', as everyone else always did, so it had been lying at the bottom of his pending tray!

The import license arrived remarkably quickly with the envelope covered with Express Post stickers. It was not for 'Cat, Siamese, female, quantity one...', but for 'His Excellency, the Governor's Siamese cat, female'! What the Ministry of Agriculture and Fisheries made of this impressive import license is not recorded. The export license arrived without comment a week before Solo was due to depart.

At about the time the cat license saga had begun, I was telephoned by Mrs Eileen Gregory of the Hong Kong and General Department of the Foreign and Commonwealth Office, who administered the Diplomatic Service in Britain's smaller residual dependent territories like Gibraltar. She wanted to know how Joan and I would like to go out to Gibraltar? We could fly out in an R.A.F. HS 125, executive jet, which would be very comfortable, or we could go by sea as most of our predecessors had done.

I did know from looking at photo albums, when we had stayed with the Governor during one of my visits to the Rock as Quartermaster General, that in the old days Governors had travelled out in one of the great luxury liners that used to plough to and fro on the South Africa route. They used to be brought ashore in the Governor's barge, and would land with full colonial pomp and ceremony at Governor's Steps. The great liners were unfortunately a thing of the past. As an ex-Quartermaster-General, it might have been appropriate to take passage in one of the Army's logistic ships, like the Sir Gallahad of future Falkland fame, which belonged to the Q.M.G.'s Department, but I hesitated because I was not sure how comfortable one would be for Joan and perhaps Solo.

Mrs Gregory sensed my uncertainty and came to my rescue:

"We're rather keen to make something of a show of your arrival for the benefit of the Spaniards, who have been spreading the rumour that a civilian governor is to be appointed, downgrading Gibraltar's military importance and thus improving their case for the return of the Rock to their sovereignty."

Realising that I might not fathom the logic of this train of thought, she continued:

"Under the Treaty of Utrecht, Gibraltar must be returned to them if and when the United Kingdom no longer needs it. As it was ceded to us as a fortress, they believe any decline in its military importance helps their case."

Before I could reply, she added;

"I've contacted the Navy and they have confirmed that they are prepared to take you and Lady Jackson out in one of Her Majesty's ships. They will let us know which one as soon as the ship programme for May is firm. It will probably be a carrier going to the Far East."

I agreed with alacrity and put the phone down with a flourish. What fun to sail out in a warship with all the traditional courtesies of the Royal Navy. I rushed through into the kitchen where Joan was doing some cooking, and told her the good news. Her face fell:

"What about Solo?"

What about Solo indeed. In my excitement I had not given her a thought. But surely the Navy would take her too: they carried pets and animal mascots, so Solo should be welcome. After all, as a governor's cat, she would be senior even to the captain's cat!

Joan was not impressed:

"Didn't you see that bit in the Press about the rabies scare. The Navy has had to put all its pets ashore."

Now that she mentioned it, I had to confess that I had seen the article, but had forgotten all about it. This, however, turned out to be irrelevant. Joan stated quite categorically that Solo could not go out by sea even if Their Lordships at the Admiralty made her an exception and granted her passage in one of their men-of-war.

Joan's view was that Solo would be quite impossible in a ship. She was hard enough to find when we wanted her at West Stowell. On board, she would have infinitely more places in which to hide, and many more reasons for seeking sanctuary. Every member of the crew would be a potential enemy from whom she must hide.

"If you want to spend the voyage searching the bowels of the ship every day for Solo, fine; but I'm not coming. And anyway how would you know that she had not fallen overboard? We would be nervous wrecks by the time we reached Gibraltar, and the crew would probably have mutinied from the strain of constant searches as well!"

And so we decided not to approach Their Lordships for special dispensation for Solo. She would have to go out by air. The only problem to be resolved was who should accompany her and look after her if she arrived ahead of us as seemed likely since we would want to shut up West Stowell before we left ourselves. This train of thought led to a very happy conclusion a few hours later.

I cannot now recall which of us thought of the solution first. We would both have liked our son and daughter to have been able to see our ceremonial arrival in Gibraltar. Our son, Nigel had left with his battalion for a tour in Hong Kong and would certainly not be able to get back for the occasion; but our daughter, Rosie was living quite near us, as I said earlier, at Barton Stacey. She put in a bid to come out as soon as she heard where we were going. She had no children as yet and so was free to do so.

Then the penny dropped. Why not ask the Engineer-in-Chief if her husband could temporarily reassume the duties of my A.D.C. for the voyage out, so that my future A.D.C. could go out ahead of us to sort out our new house staff before we arrived? As is the custom when governors change, my predecessor would be leaving about six weeks before I arrived, and the Deputy Governor would take over during the interregnum. In the interval, all the necessary staff changes would be made, any refurbishment of the governor's residency would be carried out, and so forth. My predecessor was Marshal of the Royal Air Force Sir John Grandy, so most of his personal staff were airmen and would leave with him. My soldier replacements would need time to learn their duties and get together as an efficient team under my new A.D.C.

The plan soon crystallized. The E-in-C agreed to release Captain R.J.D. Reid - 'Knobby' to us and his friends - to be my 'A.D.C. at Sea'. Rosie appointed herself lady-in-waiting to Solo for her passage by air to Gibraltar. She would fly out some days before we left and would be there to meet us when we arrived.

Their Lordships of the Admiralty nominated a Leander Class frigate, to take us out. She was not exactly what Eileen Gregory had in mind. No larger ship, however, was sailing in the direction of Gibraltar at that time, so it would be up to Captain Briggs, *Apollo*'s captain, to make us as comfortable as possible in the very limited space available in a frigate. Thank goodness, thought Joan, we are not going to try squeezing Solo in as well.

And the Air Movements Branch at the Ministry of Defence were unusually helpful. They agreed that Rosie could have an 'indulgence' passage on the twice-weekly military charter flight to Gibraltar. Solo could go with her as long as her export papers were in order and she was carried in a securely locked cat basket. She would, they assured me, be treated as an infant-in-arms and her basket would be placed in the seat next to Rosie as a carry-cot would be, and not in the hold.

I will not go into all the problems of deciding what we should take; what we should leave behind; who should look after the house while we were away; what to do about our car; who should forward our mail; and all the host of mundane details of such a move. These things are common to all Service changes of station, which thousands of sailors, soldiers and airmen undertake every year, and we had experienced on numerous occasions throughout my military career. The only person who found the business in any way extraordinary was Solo.

To Solo, packing up was the greatest fun. She was into everything, supervising the Foreign Office packers arranged for us by Eileen Gregory. There was a grave danger that she would be packed by mistake, but at the end of the day she answered her name at roll call as the cases were carried out of the house to the waiting removal van. At last everything had gone and we were left with the suitcases that were to go with us in H.M.S. *Apollo*; and Solo had her basket, feeding bowls, and a new catmint mouse to keep her amused during her flight out with Rosie.

Rosie arrived that evening, just as the telephone rang. I don't think that we will ever forget that call. Joan took it as I was carrying Rosie's suitcases upstairs for her. Soon I heard Joan calling me with an agonised tone in her voice. What could have happened?

"Solo can't go," she blurted out, "Tom is on the phone from Gib."

Tom was the unflappable and determined submariner, who had rashly accepted the appointment of Military Assistant to the new Governor, without knowing much about me or, for his peace of mind, of the existence of Solo. I had asked the First Sea Lord to provide me with a naval officer for the job because Gibraltar is predominantly a naval station, and I needed some one on my personal staff to keep me abreast with naval affairs. The Military Assistant's job is to run the Governor's private office, but, as he is the senior personal staff officer, he is also major domo of the Governor's Residence; and *ipso facto* the confidant of the Governor's wife, and, in Joan's case, of her cat as well.

This was the first of many crises that the long-suffering, but imperturbable Tom was to be faced with due to Solo's presence in our household. It appeared from what Tom could tell me over the phone that there had been one of those infuriating breakdowns in communication that are apt to occur in all walks of life. When the Joint Services Movements Staff received the request for an 'indulgence' passage for the Governor's daughter and accompanying cat, the clerk concerned, believing that 'Governors' could have anything they wanted, and that their requests should not be questioned, quickly approved the booking and allocated the seats. He or she did not check whether Dan Air, the charter air line, had a licence to carry livestock. Dan Air did not, and only revealed the fact the day before Solo was due to fly out.

Tom had to relay this unwelcome and unexpected news to West Stowell. Before ringing us he had enquired about alternative carriers, but such was the shortage of space on the few aircraft, which used to fly to Gibraltar during the siege, that no bookings were to be had for about ten days. As a long shot, he suggested that I should approach Captain James Briggs, the Captain of *Apollo*. to see whether he would give Solo a passage to Gibraltar with us in spite of the recent rabies scare. After all, her papers were in order, and she could be treated as live cargo rather than as a ship's pet as defined in the Admiralty order prohibiting pets on board H.M. Ships!

I rang James Briggs straight away. He and his wife, Barby, had

45

been to lunch with us at West Stowell only a week before so I was not speaking to a stranger. Nevertheless, there was an appreciable pause at the other end of the phone when I put my request to him in so tentative a way that he could refuse without loss of face on either side, if he felt the risks were too great.

Jas Briggs, as he is called in the Navy, where he has the reputation of being one of the finest ship handlers, came up trumps.

"I'll see what I can do. Just leave it to me," he said, and then asked, "Are her papers in order?"

I assured him that she had export and import licenses, and the total volume of paper about *her* weighed far more than both our passports and inoculation certificates put together. She was not a piece of contraband to be smuggled into Gibraltar: her papers stated clearly that she was the Governor's Cat (Designate). The Spaniards have accused Gibraltar over almost three centuries of being a smugglers' paradise, but Solo could not possibly become a *cause célèbre* and add one more straw to the camel's back of British diplomacy in the Anglo-Spanish squabble over Gibraltar.

I put the phone down at the end of our conversation with a certain sense of elation. The Navy never let anyone down as I had good reason to know. In the darkest days of 1940, I had been rescued by H.M.S. *Galatea* from the Norwegian coast after I and my Sapper troop had failed to reach Andalsnes in time for the evacuation of British troops. We had been blowing bridges to check the German advance, and could not get to the embarkation point before dawn broke and forced the ships to pull out of the fiords to avoid German air attack. *Galatea*, however, made the perilous journey back up the fiords next night and took us off. But that is another long story, and has nothing whatsoever to do with Solo.

Jas did not ring back until next morning. I had slept well, but Joan had an agonising night of anxiety, having less reason for confidence in the Navy than I had. Jas said that he had thought it wise to clear his arm with his immediate superiors. How far up the chain of command he went was never revealed. The essential fact was that Solo would not become the Governor's Cat (Manqué)!

"Solo's on," he said without any preliminaries, "just bring her down to Portsmouth with you in her basket - preferably doped - and leave her in the car when you embark. We'll do the rest!"

I asked no questions; thanked him profusely; and then drove down to the vets' to get a suitable tranquilliser to keep Solo incommunicado during her embarkation.

Joan was so relieved that she forgot all her fears about what Solo might get up to at sea. Solo, I think, must have heard my conversation with Jas. She discarded the subtitle of 'Manqué' that she had been forced to wear since Tom's telephone call, and donned 'Designate' again like a halo. Her step became lighter, her tail more erect, and her purr louder. She started growing once more into her future role, which was almost upon her.

CHAPTER 5

H.M.S. APOLLO

There are many worlds within this world, and one of them is the world of the Royal Navy. And within that world was the well defined sub-world of H.M.S. *Apollo* and Jas Briggs. In the Royal Naval world, nothing is commonplace: perfection is the only yardstick of that highly professional Service. It is a professionalism that appears effortless, as it is founded on centuries of experience, and is maintained by the constant efforts of every ship in the Fleet, trying to be, and being convinced it is the best ship in the Navy, if not in the world. I had always been aware of this epitome of professionalism since my rescue from Norway, and from my experiences in the landings in North Africa, Sicily, Italy and the Far East during the Second World War.

Solo was too doped to sense the aurora of the White Ensign as we arrived alongside the grey hull of *Apollo* in Portsmouth naval base. We wondered what her reaction would be to Jas Briggs's world when she came to: the steel instead of brick walls, shrill pipes, blaring tannoy calls, strange looking sailors, the noise of the engines and ventilator systems, the flapping of signal flags at their halyards, the smells of salt and fuel oil, the pitching of the ship, the creaking of her hull, the grey-green turbulence of the sea, and the swirling track of the wake, stretching to the horizon. Would she accept this as all part of the new world into which she was being promoted, or would she be overcome with a fit of nerves when she woke up and so disgrace us all?

Joan had other worries: what would happen if she strayed out of our cabin where she was to be confined for the voyage? She might take fright and disappear, for ever, over the side into that foaming wake. Or she might disappear into the bowels of the ship, and Jas would have to order a major search operation to find her. Worst of all, she might be so frightened that she would dart into some inaccessible place, and die there from starvation, unheard, unsung and unseen until an unpleasant aroma drew attention to her last resting place! There was plenty of stuff from which nightmares could be tailored in Joan's mind during our last night at West Stowell; but, in fact, we both slept well, mentally exhausted by the last minute hiccup over Solo's passage.

There was one fortunate circumstance about our embarkation. It was on a Saturday so that we would arrive in Gibraltar on Tuesday morning, which was the day appointed for my inauguration as Governor. Even in the Royal Navy - on shore at least - Saturday is for recreation. All self-respecting senior officers hope to be enjoying their favourite sport or pastime. The last thing that they wanted was to be giving me a ceremonial send off, so I agreed with Jas, who put the point to me on behalf of his Admiral, that the informality of a Saturday departure should be made up for by an impressive arrival at Gibraltar.

"Lots of bow wave ahead and plenty of scrambled eggs at the stern as we come up the Bay of Gibraltar; full power as we pass through the harbour entrance; and a perfect alongside so that the brow can be lowered exactly on the red carpet!" Jas promised with undisguised enthusiasm. It was to be a splendid finale to our two-and-a-half day voyage in *Apollo*.

A large Ministry of Defence Daimler drew up at the house at precisely ten o'clock on the morning of our departure to carry us to Portsmouth. As there was plenty of room in the car, we had invited our nearest neighbour, a very nice widow, Betty Yeomans, to come down to Portsmouth with us to see us off. Jas Briggs had kindly invited her to lunch in *Apollo* before we sailed in the early afternoon.

Betty had come round to our house in good time before the car arrived and quickly became involved in the saga of getting the tranquilliser down Solo before we set off. The Governor's Cat (Designate) was in no mood to co-operate. Joan held her while I tried to push the small white pill down her throat.

My reward was a couple of perforated fingers from which my blood gushed, splattering Solo's white fur. Six hands were clearly better than four when dealing with a recalcitrant cat because with Betty's help we managed to force that pill down Solo's gullet without further blood-letting.

Into the cat-basket Solo went before she could vent her anger on us; the straps holding the grill were fastened; and onto the floor in the back of the car she went between Joan's and Betty's feet. I decided to keep well out of the way by sitting alongside the driver in front of the car. The journey to our new life, and Solo's, in the Mediterranean, began.

In the last-minute rush to get away on time, we had quite forgotten Solo's aversion to cars. No sooner were we out of the drive than she started complaining in that wailing, high pitched Siamese cry.

"I don't want to go! Take me back! Let me out! Let me out! Damn you, damn you, etc..."

And with each scream she would tear at the newspaper padding in the bottom of the basket with her claws.

"The pill should soon be working," I said with totally misplaced confidence.

Solo's complaints grew more strident rather than fading away as the tranquilliser started its errand of mercy as far as we were concerned. We had completed almost half the sixty-mile journey before her language became less abusive. But even as the drug took hold she still refused to give up! Her head would sink onto her paws, and she would shake it and try yet another but decreasingly vehement protest about how unfair we were being to her.

She did not pass out completely until we were entering the Royal Dockyard gates. Her collapse, when it came, was complete; not an eyelid flickered, not a muscle twitched.

She was in the land of nod, and quite unable to catch even a glimpse of the world of the White Ensign, which she was entering, and with which she was to become all too familiar over the next

50

five years.

If this was a Saturday, I dreaded to think what a week day departure would have been like. At the Dockyard gate, an escort car was waiting to guide us to *Apollo*'s berth. As we drove past a seemingly endless line of grey hulls with Union Flags at their bows and great White Ensigns flying at their sterns, we could hear the pipes calling their ship's companies, in Army parlance, 'to attention'. I had not realised that the Royal Navy had so many ships in commission. Everything is relative: compared with the first half of the century, numbers had shrunk, but the power of those that exist today outstrips the fleets of yesteryear. The modern ships may be smaller too, but their sting is more lethal.

The Daimler pulled up at the foot of *Apollo*'s brow, or, as civilians and soldiers would call it in their ignorance, the gangway. Remembering Jas's instructions, we left Solo in her basket, fast asleep, in the back of the car to be treated as just a piece of our personal luggage. As we climbed up the brow, we were piped aboard and welcomed by Jas and the officer of the watch as we stepped down onto the deck. Knobby, our son-in-law and A.D.C. for the voyage, was hovering discreetly in the background, having embarked the day before, theoretically to make our administrative arrangements - a quite superfluous task as Jas and his team were more than capable of looking after us perfectly!

When Jas led us down to his day and night cabins under the bridge, which he had kindly put at our disposal for the voyage, I saw, out of the corner of my eye as we left the deck, a naval steward going down the brow with a very large cardboard box that had once contained packets of Kellogg's cornflakes. I thought nothing more about it: stewards and cornflakes were a natural combination that did not warrant special attention.

Jas left us to 'freshen up', as the Americans say, after inviting us to join him on the bridge for pre-lunch drinks with his Admiral. I wondered why his Admiral was not week-ending as we had agreed, but, like the cornflakes box, I did not give the question any further thought.

A discreet knock on the door a few minutes later announced

the arrival of *Apollo*'s Chief Steward, who asked politely whether we had everything we wanted. Behind him I could see that Kellogg's cornflakes box in the arms of the junior steward, whom I had seen going down the brow to the car. Before I could answer, the Petty Officer stepped into the cabin, pulling the door to behind him. Looking very respectful and in a confidential half whisper, he asked Joan,

"Where would you like your cat, my lady?"

In came the Kellogg's box carried by Steward Shackleton, Jas's personal steward, and out of it came Solo's cat basket with Solo still fast asleep inside it. Solo had embarked un-heralded and, it was to be hoped, unseen.

When the Chief Steward had left, Shackleton explained to Joan that only he and the Chief Steward knew of Solo's presence in *Apollo* and they had been sworn to secrecy. It would not do, he pointed out with measured gravity, for the tabloid press to find out that a cat had been embarked after the Admiralty had ordered all pets to be put ashore. Even though her papers, he was sure, were in order, there would be headlines proclaiming one law for senior officers and another for ratings. We could imagine them:

"Sailors protest. Top brass breaks the rules for Governor's Cat!"

"Privileges for Governor's Lady's cat!"

"Solo, the Siamese, embarked as Kellogg's Cornflakes: what a fiddle!"

Shackleton then returned to more earthy subjects: had we brought a sand box, or should he improvise one? We had, and a large bag of cat litter too, so we left him to attend to Solo's sanitary arrangements and went up to the bridge to meet the Admiral.

On the way Jas intercepted us. He had two problems on his

mind.

"You'll be meeting Admiral and Mrs Pritchard on the bridge. They're staying for lunch;" he said in almost a whisper. "He wants to meet you, because he is likely to be the next Flag Officer, Gibraltar. He doesn't want you to know this since it is usual for the First Sea Lord to tell you first."

I could only whisper back that I already knew on the grape vine, but he was quite right in that the First Sea Lord had not, as yet, written to me. I could, of course, always say 'no' to his appointment, but this was most unlikely as I did not know many senior naval officers and certainly nothing of Gwyn Pritchard's capabilities. All I knew was that he had the reputation of being a fierce disciplinarian and a stickler for detail.

"He is Admiral, Sea Training at Portland. A fortnight ago we completed our work up under his eagle eye with flying colours, I'm delighted to say," Jas continued in a slightly louder voice. "We are no longer under his command, so his excuse for coming today is to say 'Bon Voyage' to one of his recent products."

So that was why we had an admiral on board to send us off on a Saturday!

"My second problem," Jas said, returning to a whisper, "is that the Admiral knows nothing about Solo. I cleared my arm with the Chief of Staff to C-in-C Portsmouth as I am now under his command. I suggest that we just refer to her as 'the fourth member' of your party, who is in your cabin as she is not feeling very well."

I saw no reason to disagree, but both Jas and I had forgotten that, until the guests departed just before the ship sailed, we did actually have a genuine 'fourth member' - Betty Yeomans. The seeds for a mini-farce had been sown. As far as the Admiral was concerned my party, as Jas introduced us to him were myself, Joan, Knobby, and Betty.

Betty, who has since died, was a tall and very distinguished looking woman with beautiful grey hair: Joan is shorter, equally distinguished, but with dark hair and was obviously much younger. The Admiral, who did, indeed, look a bit like Captain

Bligh, did not catch the names very clearly above the electronic noises and ventilator hum on the bridge. He took Betty to be Lady Jackson, relegating Joan to the status of her companion and 'Fourth Member'.

Turning to Joan, he said: "And who are you? I'm sorry, I did not catch your name."

Joan laughed, and then explained that Betty had come down to see us off. All was well - at least until after lunch!

Jas's hospitality did justice to the White Ensign throughout our voyage, but none more so than his welcoming luncheon in *Apollo*'s ward-room. The time came all too soon to say farewell to Betty, the Admiral and his wife, Tessa. I saw Steward Shackleton go up to Jas and whisper something to him. Jas came across to me where I was standing, drinking my post-lunch cup of coffee, and said quietly:

"The 'Fourth Member' is creating!" and then nodding in the direction of the Admiral, said in a real whisper:

"We can't get him past your cabin unless you can shut her up!"

I think that I saw the Admiral look quickly at Betty, wondering what she was creating about, but I may have imagined it. I slipped out of the cabin with Shackleton to see what could be done. The Governor's Cat was certainly creating. She was making the same din that she made when she was in season and was trying to attract boy-friends. She told me in no uncertain terms what she thought of me, and was demanding to be taken home at once. It was not her fault that she was still shut in the damn cat basket. Would I kindly let her out or she would yell the whole ship down, call the press, and do all manner of disloyal things.

I had some spare tranquillisers, but our experience of the slowness of their action in the Daimler did not commend them as a solution to our immediate problem. Shackleton came up with a possible solution:

"Best turn on the ship's broadcast, Sir: that could drown the row a bit - she might even enjoy it!" And he stretched over Joan's bunk to a row of switches under the loud speaker. Out roared the latest pop music.

The decibel level of the pop group, performing at the time, did not dowse Solo's complaints entirely, but it did disguise them. Success would depend on our being able to hustle the Admiral past the cabin quickly enough to stop him realising that the letter, if not the spirit, of Admiralty orders was being broken. He had only just finished instilling respect for regulations into *Apollo*'s crew during sea training; and he was the type of Admiral - or so his reputation led me to believe - who could become a Captain Bligh at the least provocation.

I am told that Nelson so trained his fleet that all his ships' captains knew instinctively what he would want them to do in a crisis. In a good ship, the same thing is true. *Apollo* was a good ship under Jas's command. Somehow the navigating officer on the bridge sensed that there was a crisis of some kind in the ward-room below. He tested the ship's siren just at the most opportune moment, suggesting to the Admiral that he was leaving his departure a bit late.

As the Admiral emerged on the deck, his departure was further hastened by the sight of the dock-side crane preparing to lift off the brow. The question in my mind was whether it would accelerate his passage past the porthole of Joan's cabin enough to stop him distinguishing between Solo's moans and the voice of the singer, who was currently Top of the Pops?

Nail biting seconds passed, and then there were two blasts on the siren, indicating that *Apollo* would be turning to port as she left her berth. We were in luck. The blasts coincided with the admiral's passage past the vital porthole. All was well as he broke into a slight trot, heading for the quarterdeck. When he reached it, he returned Jas's salute, and, with recovered dignity, went down the brow.

Even the crane drive seemed to be intent on saving Solo. Before the Admiral's feet actually touched *terra firma*, he started to lift the brow away and *Apollo*'s engines started to turn, easing her away from the quay. It was as if the ship was saying to the 'Fourth Member':

"We'll have him ashore, Solo, before he finds out; don't you worry."

Apollo was as good as her word, although she got no thanks from Solo, who looked upon the whole voyage as a very unpleasant experience, whereas we enjoyed every minute of it. The ship's company could not have made us feel more at home. When I look at the picture of *Apollo*. which Jas gave us just before we left the ship, I always feel part of her: she was 'our ship'. Even *Fearless*, of Falklands fame, which took us home almost five years later, does not fill such an important niche in our hearts for one simple reason: Solo went home by air, as I will recount later, so the 'Fourth Member' was missing, which made all the difference.

Joan was very anxious about two things: the possibility of rough weather in the Bay of Biscay, and the danger of Solo escaping and plunging over the side to find Davy Jones's Locker, or to swim back to her beloved West Stowell. Neither happened. The weather was grey and uninteresting with only a slight swell running all the way to Gibraltar; and Solo failed to make her escape from the prison devised for her.

To make us as comfortable as possible, Jas had given us his captain's accommodation that lay just under the bridge. It consisted of his day and night cabins with a bath room and small passage in between them. Joan had his night cabin, and I slept in the 'Dutch Admiral's bunk' pulled down in the day cabin. Why, you may well ask, the 'Dutch Admiral's bunk'? Apparently the *Leander* Class frigates were designed to operate with NATO naval forces, which often involved embarking NATO admirals for inter-Allied operations. These were more often than not Dutchmen, as Holland provides the third largest naval contingent for the defence of the Eastern Atlantic, North Sea and English Channel. On this occasion it was a British General, who made use of this little bit of forethought by the naval ship designers at Bath.

A far more important feature of the captain's suite of cabins as far as Solo and we were concerned, was the existence of no less than three doors between the night cabin and the freedom of the outer deck with its potential attractions and dangers for Solo. She was incarcerated in the night cabin for the whole voyage, and we had a strict drill for never opening more than one of the doors at a time. To leave her cabin, Joan would shut her door into the passage past the bathroom before opening the door into the day cabin; and the day cabin door onto the deck was never opened unless the door into the bathroom passage was shut. I am thankful to record that, although there were one or two inevitable lapses of memory on our part, Solo never managed to exploit them.

Solo had many and varied reasons for thinking nothing of *Apollo*. She had been deprived of the thing most precious to her: her cat-flap. Push where she would, no panel would open. To add insult to injury, she was back using a sand box, which was like asking a teenager to wear nappies! These things all hurt her dignity, and were a constant cause of complaint. As the ship's company were, in theory, not to know that there was a cat on board, we had to turn on the ship's broadcast so frequently to disguise her complaints that I am sure the rumour must have gone round the ship that Joan was an avid pop music fan.

And Solo did not think much of the ship's catering either. Steward Shackleton did his very best to please her to no avail. Nothing was right. She preferred her mistress's cooking, and disliked naval messing. In any case, she was used to working up an appetite with a little mousing, which she was now debarred from doing. The whiff of fuel oil and the pitching of the ship did not help her appetite either. Food was the last thing she wanted until she got her sea-legs. Furthermore, she was probably suffering a hangover from the tranquilliser as well. Whatever the cause, she was not at her Siamese best as she kept on reminding us with plaintive cries throughout the voyage.

We did, however, learn one thing new about Solo that she had in common with Jas Briggs: both adored Marmite on toast. Jas came down to have tea with us on our last afternoon on board to brief us on the arrangements for our arrival. Shackleton, knowing his master's likes and dislikes, provided his favourite dish as well as daintily cut sandwiches and cream cakes. Solo appeared as soon as Jas helped himself lavishly to the Marmite, and told him with a loud and endearing purr that she would like some too! Jas presented her with a very small square of Marmited toast just for fun, expecting her to turn up her nose in horror at such a strong tasting morsel. Not a bit of it: she wopped it down and asked for more.

Shackleton was quick to take the hint. A little Marmite on her last supper on board made all the difference to Solo's view of his cooking and of her voyage in *Apollo*. Joan noted it too for future use when Solo was off her food as she was apt to be if hunting was good and she had eaten too many mice.

All good things, and bad ones too, come to an end. As far as Joan and I were concerned, we were quite sad, though inwardly excited as *Apollo* turned off Cape St Vincent towards the Strait of Gibraltar on our last night at sea. Solo, on the other hand, was delighted when the ship stopped pitching as we left the Atlantic. She wolfed her Marmite flavoured cod supper that Shackleton had specially prepared for her, and settled down on Joan's bunk. She was determined to have a good night's rest so that she would be looking her best for our arrival next morning and the removal of 'Designate' from her title!

The arrival of a new governor in any of Britain's dependent territories causes a great deal of work and anxiety for a lot of people behind the scenes. The Deputy Governor, Robin O'Neill of the Diplomatic Service, had been acting-Governor since Sir John Grandy left, and was responsible for all the arrangements. The Chief Minister, Speaker of the House of Assembly, the Commissioner of Police, and the Heads of the Navy, Army and Air Force in Gibraltar, had important parts to play. Most of the detailed co-ordination of the programme fell on the shoulders of Commander Tom Le Marchand, my Military Assistant; and all the domestic arrangements, including Solo's secret move from *Apollo* to her future residence, were in the hands of Captain Andy Craig, Royal Engineers, my A.D.C. ashore.

The programme, covering my stepping ashore as the new Queen's Representative, my swearing-in at the House of Assembly by the Chief Justice, and our arrival at the Convent, the Governor's

Residence in Gibraltar - why it is called the Convent, I will be recounting later - had to be worked out in the minutest detail like any other Royal occasion. Timing was crucial because Gibraltar is so small that you cannot slip off time if you are too early, nor catch it up if you are likely to be late.

During our voyage out *Apollo*'s communicators had been kept busy receiving amendments to our programme, and more importantly to my inaugural speech, which had to be just right: providing assurance to the people of Gibraltar of H.M.G.'s continuing support in their confrontation with Spain: and yet not gratuitously offensive to the Spaniards, who had it in their power to continue the 15th, and most recent, Siege of the Rock almost indefinitely.

Mixed up amongst all the official communications were messages about our own family problems: how Rosie was to join us at sea to take part in our arrival and be very much noticed as we were very proud of her; and how Solo was to get ashore and reach the Convent without anyone noticing her at all, particularly any of the press, who might be nosing round for a human, or rather animal, interest story.

Before we left Portsmouth, Rosie had given us the hat and dress that she intended to wear at the inauguration so that they would not be crushed in her suitcases that went out with her by air. We had been assured by Jas that *Apollo*'s helicopter would be able to pick her up from the Rock, and fly her out to the ship in the Strait just before we turned into the Bay of Gibraltar. 'The best laid plans of mice and men, etc....' *Apollo*'s helicopter went sick at the last moment! So there was Rosie ashore, while her carefully chosen hat and dress were in *Apollo* at sea!

More signals must have passed between *Apollo* and the naval signal station on Windmill Hill about that hat and dress than all the amendments to my speech and our programme. Should they be sent ashore or should Rosie join them, as originally intended at sea? But how?

The Royal Navy is never at a loss in a crisis involving a very young and attractive member of the female sex. The Queen's

Harbour-Master gallantly strode to Rosie's rescue, offering to her the option of going out with him in his launch to *Apollo* or for him to pick up her essential garments from the ship and to bring them ashore to her. He did warn her that the journey out to *Apollo* in the Strait might be a bit choppy and not very comfortable in his smallish launch.

Rosie chose to join her clothes in *Apollo*. I saw no problem in her doing so. Jas said he would bring *Apollo* close in to the south-eastern side of Europa Point, the southern tip of the Rock, in the early morning mist before any of the inhabitants were likely to be scanning the sea for the arrival of their new governor. When the Queen's Harbour-Master's launch came alongside, Rosie might have a bit of difficulty, I thought, in jumping from the bobbing launch onto the rolling gangway, which I assumed Jas would lower for her. Rosie, herself, had no qualms about the operation, but she did take the precaution of wearing jeans and not a skirt for the journey out to us.

Soon after daybreak we saw the great Rock looming up through a low sea mist, majestic and forbidding, and looking every bit the strategically important guardian of the Strait. Both the ancient Pillars of Hercules were visible from *Apollo*'s bridge, sticking up through the cotton wool blanket lying over the sea: British Gibraltar to port and Spanish Ceuta to starboard.

Joan spotted the Harbour-Master's launch first as it emerged from the mist.

"There she is!" Joan cried, waving excitedly to Rosie, who was sitting in the stern of the pitching boat. "How's she going to get on board?"

I had not noticed that Jas had done nothing about lowering *Apollo*'s gangway for her. The solution to the problem was soon apparent. Two ratings threw down a rope ladder. I saw a look of horror on Rosie's face as she too realised that climbing it was the only way up to us. Brave girl that she is, she did not hesitate and made a successful leap onto the bottom rung of the first rope ladder she had ever tried to climb. By the time she reached the top, she wished her hat and dress had been brought to her on shore!

Rosie was not piped aboard as we had been, but received a rousing cheer from the ship's company as they helped her over the last few feet onto the deck, exhausted but proud of herself.

Disembarking Solo was to be the exact reverse of her embarkation: administration of tranquilliser; into cat basket, and Kellogg's cornflake box; down the brow with the rest of our luggage after we had left for the House of Assembly; loaded into a naval baggage wagon; then off to the Convent where she would arrive *incognito* and unconscious; and finally come to, we hoped, in our future bedroom some time after we reached the Convent so that we and no one else would introduce her to her new surroundings. We had no wish to go through a repeat of her arrival at West Stowell.

Nor did I intend to lose the end of my finger again, administering the tranquilliser. With a little bit of judicious flattery about how good Joan was at giving medicine to sick animals, I persuaded her to push the pill down Solo's throat while I held her firmly wrapped up in a towel. This time no blood was drawn in the dosing process; Solo was pushed protesting into her hated cat basket; and we turned on the broadcast in a final vain endeavour to keep her presence in *Apollo* secret.

The only snag in Solo's disembarkation was Shackleton's discovery that some tidy minded person had jettisoned the Kellogg's box. The only thing he could find to replace it was a similar box advertising a well known brand of toilet paper. Any nosey member of the Press, who decided to examine our baggage might well have concluded that the new Governor thought Gibraltar was so primitive that he had to bring out his own supply of this vital commodity! And so it was that Solo was to disembark as loo rolls instead of cornflakes.

She was, of course, blissfully unaware of her transformation into His Excellency' Cat. She went through the transformation like a caterpillar turning into a butterfly: caterpillar in *Apollo*; unconscious chrysalis in her cat-basket; and a butterfly when she woke up in the Convent. Just as much was to happen to us in the three hours of her metamorphosis.

After embarking Rosie, Jas took *Apollo* back out into the Strait ready to make her high speed run up the Bay and entry into Gibraltar's great torpedo-proof naval harbour, which once used to be home to the British Mediterranean and Home Fleets in the days of Empire. Lots of bow wave and scrambled eggs, as Jas had described his proposed use of full power, was fine when on a straight course, but, when turning at speed, frigates lean over like motor-cyclists on a bend. To the watchers on shore this was a splendid sight, but for us below decks, getting dressed up in our ceremonial finery, there were obvious hazards.

My full-dress must have been the most impracticable rig ever devised for disembarking from one of Her Majesty's ships. White starched tunic, which showed the slightest crease or mark; skin tight blue trousers with a broad scarlet stripe down the side that fastened under the instep of my Wellington boots, making movement almost as difficult as a knight's in full armour; heavy gold aiguilettes of an A.D.C. General to the Queen that could catch on any of the many fittings that stick out in a warship; sword carried on slings from the belt under my tunic that could trip me up; and, worst of all, spurs on my heels that were certainly not designed for going down ships companionways or brows. The whole ensemble was potentially a cartoonist's dream.

We were all assembled in Jas's day cabin as *Apollo* started her final run-in up the Bay. Rosie decided that she must have a cup of coffee to recover from her ordeal. The thought had barely entered her head than Shackleton, with the perfect steward's anticipation, appeared with coffee on a silver tray.

Rosie did not know it, but that tray was to be her means of getting her own back on Jas for her unladylike ascent from the Queen's Harbour-Master's launch to *Apollo*'s deck.

We were sipping our welcome cups of coffee somewhat nervously, wishing that the next three hours would soon be over, when Jas made his turn towards the harbour entrance. Crash - the coffee pot, milk jug and sugar basin all shot off the tray in Shackleton's hands and landed on the Cabin floor. Jas heard the crash on the bridge above, and rushed down to see what had happened. Pushing his head through the curtains across the doorway, he asked.

"Everything all right?"

"Not really," replied Rosie, as quick as a flash; "My father's got coffee all down the back of his white tunic: he wont be able to turn round all day!"

Poor Jas's face fell. In fact, the coffee, by the grace of God, had missed us all. Rosie and Jas were quits!

It was time to take our places on the bridge wing so that people could see us as we came alongside the berth where the red carpet was ready for our landing. Jas was true to his word, and also demonstrated why he is known as one of the best ship handlers in the Navy. He came through the South Entrance at speed and brought *Apollo* to a standstill at exactly the right spot and on time to the minute. The whole thing was done with the minimum orders, no fuss and not a bump as *Apollo* settled alongside her designated berth.

While we made our way down to the quarterdeck without sword or spur induced disaster, the brow was swung into position by the dock-side crane, and we said farewell to our temporary home, which we had come to love. Some years later, in 1988 to be precise, we had a Christmas card from Jas, telling us that *Apollo* had been sold to Pakistan:

"Sad, but better than some breakers yard," he wrote. We were sad too. *Apollo* meant a lot to us and to Solo too.

The journey down the brow was just as hazardous as I expected. The slats were just nicely placed to catch my spurs! I went down crab-wise, and did not trip up.

It might be thought that as soon as I stepped ashore, Solo could have wiped the 'Designate' from her title. This was not so. Until I had been sworn in, I was still only a General and not the Governor. The point was made after Joan and I had shaken hands with all the dignitaries on the reception line - the Chief Justice, the Speaker, the Chief Minister, the Leader of the Opposition, the three Heads of the Armed Services, the Commissioner of Police, and their wives. Instead of the band of the resident battalion playing the appropriate number of bars of the National Anthem for Her Majesty's Representative, they played the 'General Salute' as the Naval, Army and R.A.F. guards of honour presented arms when I mounted the saluting dais on the dock-side. I was still only 'Designate' myself.

One of the messages sent to *Apollo* while we were still at sea by Tom Le Marchand, was a request that I should spend as long as reasonably possible inspecting the three guards of honour so that the V.I.P.s would have enough time to scramble into their cars and reach their seats in the House of Assembly before we arrived. Distances are so short on the Rock, as I have already remarked, that we might well beat some of them to it even though we would be taking a more circuitous route to slip off time.

I did as I was told, and stopped to speak to more than the usual number of sailors, soldiers and airmen in each guard, asking the obvious questions of where they came from, whether they were married, and how they liked being stationed on the Rock? As a generalisation the married men and their wives liked living in Gibraltar: there was plenty of sun, their quarters were comfortable, the schools were good, and their standard of living was higher than it would have been in England. The single men were more divided: if they were sportsmen they enjoyed Gibraltar where every conceivable sport was played to keep them busy; some were bored and said that they preferred the excitement of being shot at in Northern Ireland to being cooped up on the Rock; but the majority were just neutral, though they all missed the bright lights of a large city.

Remembering that the British soldier will never confess to liking a station, let alone telling a General that he does, I was not too disconcerted by the 'wingeing Poms', as the Australians aptly call most of us Britons. Nevertheless, I did take note of the single men's remarks about boredom; about lack of available women due to the closed frontier that shut them off from the red light district of La Linea just over the border in Spain; and about the inevitable punch-ups with the locals, who could, at times, be unfriendly, and with the crews of visiting warships in the many pubs that abound in Gibraltar, as in any other garrison town.

The point about still being just a General was rubbed in during our drive to the House of Assembly by the absence of the Crown and Governor's flag on the Daimler. The slightly adverse impression that I gained from my inspection of the guards of honour was soon swept away by the genuine warmth of our reception as we drove through the streets. People on the pavements clapped and waved, and the school children, who had obviously been let out of their classrooms early for the occasion, fluttered small Union Jacks with great enthusiasm. What we did not know was that the Spanish Press had been spreading rumours that I was to be the last British Governor before the colony was taken back by Spain. That was enough to make every Gibraltarian turn out to express loyalty to the British Crown.

The contrast between our reception by the Services and by the civilian population never changed during our stay in Gibraltar. To the former, I was just another General - their C-in-C, indeed, but nothing more. To the latter, I was more than even the Queen's Representative: I was their protector against Spain. In short, I was just ordinary to the British sailors, soldiers and airmen, but very special to the Gibraltarians, although, as yet, they did not know me. They were acutely interested in what Joan and I would be like. Would we stand up and fight Whitehall, Westminster and Madrid on their behalf, or would we be neutral in the struggle with Spain? On this, our first day in Gibraltar, they were prepared to give us the benefit of every doubt to spite the Spaniards.

The swearing in ceremony was impressive in its simplicity. As I mounted the dais beneath the Royal Coat of Arms, I found myself flanked by the Chief Justice, Sir John Spry, a tall judicial figure in full-bottomed wig and scarlet robes; and by the morning-coated Mr Speaker, Alfredo Vasquez (now Sir Alfred, knighted in 1988 for his many years as Gibraltar's Speaker). The mace lay on the table in front of me in the charge of the Clerk to the House, the late Paul Garbarino; in the well of the chamber were the Government and opposition benches; and behind them was the public gallery, packed for the occasion with invited V.I.P.s and guests of the Members of the House.

The actual swearing in went in a dream as far as I was concerned. I might as well have been Solo in her loo roll box, and just as tranquillised! I heard myself speaking the oaths, but it did not sound like me. Then there was a roll of drums and the Port Sergeant, resplendent in the uniform of the Gibraltar Regiment, handed the Keys of the Fortress of Gibraltar to the Deputy Governor, who, until that moment, had been Acting Governor. Robin O'Neill took them with a flourish and a rattle; turned with unusually military precision for a member of the Diplomatic Service; and handed them to me with another flourish and rattle.

In the back of my mind, I remembered just in time a note that Tom had written in manuscript on my brief for the ceremony, 'Don't drop them; they're damn heavy!' In spite of his warning I nearly did so. They weigh half a stone, which you soon find out when you salute with them, as a field-marshal does with his baton. How General Elliott, the Governor during the Great Siege of 1778-82, managed to carry them on his belt at all times and went to bed with them at night, I will never understand. Incidentally, the name 'Port Sergeant' refers to 'Port' as 'Gate' and not to the wine! He used to be in charge of the gates of the fortress.

As Joan and I walked out of the House of Assembly onto the steps of the Piazza, the guns at Devil's Gap Battery started firing a seventeen gun salute; the Gibraltar Regiment guard of honour with colours on parade gave the Royal salute; and the National Anthem rang out. I realised that I was now the 52nd British Governor of the Rock. Solo had by then reached the Convent, and was demanding that Genelia, Joan's future personal maid, should let her out of her cat basket at once. She was now His Excellency's Cat and should be treated with the respect that was her due. Genelia was wise enough not to listen to her demands.

CHAPTER 6

FIRST DAYS AT THE CONVENT

Why, Solo might have asked, is the Governor's residence called the 'Convent', and not 'Government House'? When the Anglo-Dutch Confederate Fleet under Admiral Sir George Rooke took the Rock from Spain in 1704, the most prestigious building was the Franciscan friary, completed in 1531. The Franciscans are an open Roman Catholic order, whose vocation is to minister to the poor; and so in the 16th Century they built their friary and imposing chapel in the open ground in the southern half of the city. The Spanish name for a monastery inhabited by monks is either 'Monasterio' or 'Convento', and the latter was misunderstood and mispronounced by the Protestant British soldiery, who nick-named it the 'Convent'. No nuns have ever lived there, although Solo was to experience the presence of the Grey Lady - the Convent ghost - in its corridors, as I will recount later.

At first, the British Governors were content to share the building with the Abbot and the few monks, who had stayed when the rest of the Spanish inhabitants fled to the mainland to escape from the brutality of the Royal Navy's landing parties, exercising their 18th Century right and practice of plundering captured cities. But incompatibilities in military and monastic modes of life, and Catholic and Protestant antagonism, inevitably proved too much for the arrangement to last. The monks gave up the unequal struggle and left for Spain, sadly abandoning the Convent to the Governors, whose residence it has been ever since. But back to our arrival ....

The Daimler, now flying the Governor's Union Jack, emblazoned with the arms of Gibraltar, carried us from the House

67

of Assembly southward through Main Street, still lined with happy, flag waving school children, to the Convent. As it drew up at the front entrance, the Governor's Guard, provided by the garrison battalion - then the 2nd Queen's Regiment - turned out, and gave another Royal Salute. After inspecting it, I escorted Joan through the rather dark entrance hall, which was a bit like an arched tunnel, and through into the cloisters beyond. In the 16th Century, gate ways and entrances to important buildings had to be defensible, and the Convent's was no exception.

The acting Chief Steward of the Convent, Sergeant Feeney, who had served in the Convent for some fifteen years, met us and introduced us to the twenty-two members of the staff: stewards, cooks, footmen, maids, laundresses, gardeners, drivers and security policemen. Our own Chief Steward, Chief Petty Officer John Partington, could not join us for about three months as he was serving in H.M.S. *Devonshire* and could not be released immediately. Sergeant Feeney was standing in for him, and did an excellent job in helping us to find our feet in our new and yet very ancient home. We were to get to know those twenty-two faces very well indeed, but, on first acquaintance, they were just a blur after all the people we had met since stepping off *Apollo* three hours earlier.

Introductions over, we were ushered up to our private suite of rooms on the seaward side of the Convent with a view across the naval dockyard and harbour to Algeciras on the Spanish side of the Bay of Gibraltar. On the table in the centre of our bedroom was the cat basket with Solo still fast asleep inside, totally oblivious of her new surroundings. As we were due to meet all the Ministers and their wives in the garden for drinks in a quarter of an hour, we tidied ourselves up quickly and tip-toed out of the room so as not to waken her until we could supervise her introduction to the Convent.

Drinks outside on the shady lawns was a rewarding occasion. The warmth of our reception by the Ministers and their wives was unmistakably genuine, and we were grateful for it. I think that it was from this moment onwards that I felt a total dedication to Gibraltar and the Gibraltarians, which will remain with me all my life. It was probably a reflex action triggered by their equal dedication to Her Britannic Majesty, and to their determination to stay British in spite of the years of spiteful Spanish political and economic harassment that they had suffered since the Queen's post-coronation visit in 1954.

Nevertheless, the Gibraltarians were, and still are, highly suspicious of the Foreign Office mandarins. They know that there are many people in Whitehall and Westminster, who would place improvement in Anglo-Spanish relations before the wishes of the people of Gibraltar. They suspect that Gibraltar is seen in the corridors of power as an accident of history - which, of course, it is - and an out-dated imperial anachronism that should be dispensed with as decently as possible when a suitable opportunity arises. The point was made to me by Dorothy Ellicott, a former member of the Legislative Council and in her eighties:

"You know the Spaniards were saying that Sir John Grandy (my predecessor) would be the last British Governor of the Rock. Now you've come, and we are all delighted. You won't sell us down the river will you?"

I assured her that there was no possibility of my doing so; and I hoped that I sounded convincing, although in the back of my mind I was far from certain. I, too, knew that our foreign policy has been aptly described as the pragmatic pursuit of Britain's enlightened self-interest. The 'enlightened' officials in the Foreign and Commonwealth Office, who had supervised the dismantlement of the Empire, were not very likely to fight particularly hard to retain one of its last remaining outposts.

Fortunately, Andy Craig, my A.D.C., came up to me before I gave my suspicions away, and asked me if I had Solo's papers. The Rock's vet had arrived to give her the statuary anti-rabies booster injection, given to all animals entering Gibraltar. I handed him my brief-case keys, telling him what to look for. I thought no more about Solo until our guests had gone and we went in for lunch with only our personal staff and their wives present.

Apart from being rather overawed by the great dining-room, the walls of which recorded almost thirteen hundred years of

Gibraltar's history, we relaxed and metaphorically put our feet up with old friends. All had gone well, and I was now able to congratulate them all on the success of their arrangements, and thank them for their efforts on our behalf. I spoke just too soon.

Sergeant Feeney came in and whispered to the A.D.C. that the Governor's cat was behaving in a most unladylike way, swearing at poor Mr Baker, the Colony's official vet, through the wire grill of her cat basket. He would like Joan or me to help calm her down!

When I reached the bedroom I could hear her giving poor Mr Baker a piece of her mind in high-pitched Siamese:

"I don't like Gibraltar!"

"I don't like you, or any of you ***** vets!"

"Take me back to West Stowell at once!"

"No - I wont be quiet!"

"I tell you, I've had my rabies injection."

Seeing me enter the room irritated her all the more. As usual it was completely my fault: I had told her that Gibraltar was a lovely place, which it certainly was not. I had tricked her into coming out in that dreadful *Apollo*, and now look what was happening. And what right had this Mr Baker to give her another anti-rabies injection anyway?

In fact, the whole performance was an act. She was still too dopey to put up much of a fight as I lifted her gingerly out of the cat-basket. I doubt if she felt the injection. She just objected to strangers on principle, and to all vets in particular.

We decided to keep her in our private suite for a few days until she settled down and got to know some of the staff. We had to re-impose the tiresome door-closing routine that we had used in *Apollo*. The outer door of the suite was never to be opened unless the inner doors were closed and vice versa. And, of course, the hated sand-box had to be re-introduced, and frequently changed in the warm Gibraltar weather!

During her incarceration Solo worked out in her own mind her personal code of conduct, befitting her new status. She knew that I had to act as the Sovereign would wish and expect me to do as her Representative in Gibraltar. She also knew that we all had to take routine security precautions.

Although bowing and curtseying to Governors, except on very formal occasions, had died out, some of the old world protocol remained. For instance, His Excellency always goes first, ahead of his wife and other ladies; he is invariably served first at meals; and the National Anthem is played on his arrival at major social functions, the theatre, sporting events and military parades. Security precautions are constant, but not obtrusive.

Solo, of course, knew that there were Corgies in Buckingham Palace, and she assumed that there must be royal cats too. She dreamt up five rules of protocol and security that she believed they would expect her to follow:

1. Food must always be fresh; no left-overs were acceptable to the Governor's cat.

2. Food must be on the table in Joan's bathroom, and never on the floor where the ants could get it. The table legs had to stand in special, water filled, anti-ant traps.

3. At night she must always sleep between us for protection, and never at the end of the bed as we tried to make her do.

4. No one must pick her up unless invited to do so by her signalling assent by lying down first.

5. And be sure to remember Easter Bunny's tactical lessons on the indirect approach: never walk in a straight line from A to B; always take cover behind every available piece of furniture, tree, bush, or flower bed on the way in case there were terrorists about.

I must admit that she seemed to find it easier to follow her cat-made protocol than I found following a Governor's rules of etiquette and sensible security. It took me a long time to remember to go in front of Joan. She was very good and used to give me an unobtrusive nudge when I forgot.

Being served first was perhaps easier because it just happened, but it was far more hazardous than I had realised at first. At dinner parties away from the Convent, it was often difficult to decide how to tackle some Mediterranean dish that I had never met before. And even in the Convent, there were the risks in cutting first into one of the chef's prize meringue creations that could shatter across the table if I was clumsy!

Eventually Joan and I decided that we would have two sanctuaries where we could be ourselves, free of protocol. The first was our suite, although this was only a partial retreat, because Joan's maid, Genelia, and my batman, Sergeant Andrews of the Irish Guards, were free to come and go as their duties required. The other was the Governor's private cottage on an inaccessible ledge about a thousand feet up on the southern end of the Rock with magnificent views of Morocco to the south, of the Strait and the Atlantic to the west, and across the Mediterranean to the east. None of the staff, or anyone else for that matter, was allowed up there when we were using it. Only our resident sea gulls and the occasional ape were welcome.

The day came when we decided that 'Little Miss Solo', as the staff called her at first, should be allowed to inspect the Convent on her own. The building is best described for what it is: a 450 year old monastery and a cat's paradise, in which Solo could make herself responsible for the 'good order and military discipline' amongst all the small creatures that inhabit the nooks, crannies, skirting boards, and other dwelling-places that abound in such old and historic buildings.

The heart of the Convent is the square cloisters in its centre, around which it is built. The whole of the north side used to be occupied by the large Franciscan chapel, but during the Great Siege of 1778-82 the western end, nearest the sea and hence to the Spanish bombarding ships, was blown down. It was never rebuilt entirely. The Governors took the opportunity after the siege to reconstruct the damaged western third of the building as a ballroom, level with the upper floor of the rest of the Convent and with a supper-room below. The old pillars of the original entrance, with Franciscan Knots carved on them, can still be seen in the stables, now used as garages, at the west end. The remaining two thirds of the chapel, which had been used as a store house during the siege, were refurbished as the garrison church, called King's Chapel today. Amongst the many historic artifacts in King's Chapel is the original silver Communion plate donated by Queen Anne soon after the Rock's capture in 1704.

On the ground floor of the remaining three sides of the cloisters are the offices of the Governor and his immediate staff, conference rooms, communication facilities and so forth. On their upper floor are the main public rooms: dining-room, two drawing-rooms, the main guest suites, and the kitchens. The Governor's private suite is on the top floor of the 'New Wing', built in about 1870, when Lord Napier of Magdala was Governor, as an extension on the western side of the old building. Below on the ground floor of the 'New Wing', with immediate access to the swimming pool and garden, is the Royal suite, which has at times, particularly just before the First World War, been occupied by Kings, Queens, Princes and Princesses of most of Europe's Royal Houses.

The visits of Royalty over the years have resulted in the gardens being filled with exotic trees, each with a heavy bronze plaque, commemorating the occasions. The latest tree in our time marked the visit of the Prince and Princess of Wales at the start of their honeymoon in 1982. The oldest had no royal plaque. It is the famous dragon tree, reputed to be over a thousand years old, so it could have been planted in Moorish times. It has a strange beauty in its stark ugliness, and looks like a vast multi-armed cactus candelabrum with tufts of long, barbed, sword-like leaves at the end of each arm where the candle holders should be.

The gardens are about three acres in size, which, in Gibraltar where most people have to content themselves with window boxes, is very large. It is especially so, considering that it is, today, in the heart of the City where flat land is so scarce, Fortunately, for our peace of mind, it is surrounded by a high stone wall, which we hoped was Solo-proof on the inside and dog-proof on the outside. It is full of exotic plants and was carefully tended in our time by Lee Gray, a Jamaican, and Carol-Anne his English wife, who both did sterling work coping with the water shortages and burning sun in summer, and the howling gales and deluges of rain in winter.

From Solo's point of view, the gardens rivalled those of West Stowell not only as hunting grounds, but as an amusement park as well. The principal denizen was Fred, the tortoise, who kept her and us amused for hours. He was not afraid of cats, or humans for that matter. When he saw Solo he would charge her as fast as his short legs would carry him. She, for her part, would jump on his shell and try to pat his head if he stuck it out. As he rarely obliged her, she would then try to turn him over, but he was just too heavy for her and usually made his escape back into his favourite flower bed when she tired of playing with him.

Gibraltar is on one of the main bird migration routes between Europe and Africa. In spring and autumn the gardens would be the resting place for many small birds, making their long inter-continental journeys. Regrettably, Solo did occasionally catch one or two of them, probable too exhausted to spot her. Her prime target, replacing the pigeons of West Stowell as her safari ambition, were the local colony of large swifts that were with us in the summer months. They never settled on the ground, but often came dangerously near to the sweep of her claws as they dived across the lawns after insects. She never caught one to my knowledge, but it was not for want of trying.

The birds that intrigued us most, but were far beyond Solo's reach or even vision, were the large birds of prey that used to soar high up above the Rock, using its thermals to gain height for their passage across the Strait. The great honey buzzards were often attacked by our local gulls. Feathers would fly, but the buzzards made no change of course and flew majestically on as if nothing had happened.

Although Solo spent a lot of time in the garden, I think her favourite room inside the Convent - and mine - was the dining-room. We would both sit for hours there, she watching the numerous mouse holes, and I studying the greatest display of the Rock's history concentrated in one room. It used to be the monks' refectory, and had an atmosphere of timelessness about it. How many monks used to use it is uncertain, but today the great table, stretching down the centre of the room, seats twenty-six at formal dinner parties.

The names and coats of arms of all the Governors of Gibraltar - Moorish, Spanish and British - are displayed around the walls. The eight hundred years of Moorish rule is recorded on metal scrolls fixed to the panelling around the three bay windows, looking out onto the gardens. The two and a half centuries of the Spanish occupation are represented by the crests of all their Governors, painted on small round shields over the arches of the three windows. But the most imposing of all are the much larger shields, lances and pennants, of almost three centuries of British Governors displaying their coats of arms. They circle the room, just below the ancient timbers of the roof, which are unobstructed by a ceiling.

Those arms gave me my fascination for Gibraltar's history, and taught me a lot about British history as well. For instance, just under the British governors' shields are the Royal Standards of the British monarchs, who have held sovereignty over the Rock. I had no idea that they had changed so often over the centuries.

On Queen Anne's standard, the Leopards of England are halved with the Lion of Scotland in the top left and bottom right quarters, and the Fleur de Lys of France and the Irish Harp occupy the other two. The Georges had the arms of Hanover emblazoned in the centre of their standards. When Victoria came to the throne, she could not, as a woman under Salic Law, be Queen of Hanover, so the Hanovarian arms disappear, and the Leopards of England and the Scottish Lion are given a full quarter each at the expense of the Fleur de Lys of France, which disappeared too in 1801. The only recent change seems to have been the replacement of the winged and topless female figure of the Victorian style Irish harp with the plain gaelic version on Queen Elizabeth II's standard.

Some of the British Governors' arms were more note worthy than others. There is one shield with the 'bar sinister' across the Royal Standard, belonging to the Lord George Beauclerk, descended from the Duke of St Albans, a son of Charles II and Nell Gwyn. There is another Royal Standard with the white tab across the top, carried by Queen Victoria's father, the Duke of Kent, who had been Governor for just a year when the garrison mutinied against his over-strict Prussian style of discipline in 1802. He was recalled. Although he remained titular governor for the rest of his life, he never set foot on the Rock again: the Lieutenant Governors carried on the administration, but without the governor's salary, which still went to the Duke!

The pictures on the walls were equally interesting as they depict the original capture of the Rock from Spain and the Great Siege. The most intriguing of all are the small contemporary portraits of the men who were the principal characters of the Great Siege: Mr Sentence, the Ordnance Store-Keeper, round and chubby; Mr Dacre, the Agent Victualler, austere and incorruptible; Major Cunningham, the Town Major, looking rather harassed, note book in hand; the Chaplain, the Reverend Chalmers, very young and with an almost child-like countenance; the sly looking Mr Sweetland, the Collector of Revenues; the bibulous Captain Carr of the 24th of Foot, who clearly liked the good things of life, and two hard professional looking infantry brigadiers.

Amongst these relatively unimportant, though colourful, personalities are portraits by the same artist of the four men, who, apart from General Elliott, the C-in-C, did most to secure the British victory: Colonel Green and Lieutenant Skinner, the two Royal Engineers, who organised the constant repair and strengthening of the fortifications so that they withstood the four years of Franco-Spanish artillery bombardment; and Colonel Phipps and Captain Innes, their Gunner colleagues, whose ingenuity provided the battle-winning, red-hot shot that destroyed the Spanish bombarding ships.

When we first let Solo wander out from our private rooms, fear of the unknown acted as a restraining influence on her curiosity. You could see her rolling out her mental ball of string behind her to make sure that she could find her way back to safety. Footsteps of any kind would send her scuttling home to our suite. Nonetheless, we realised that this would be but a passing phase in her life. It would not be long before we would have to start worrying about the saying: curiosity kills the cat. Solo was super-curious and was always looking for the end of every rainbow, especially if she thought there was a mouse-hole to be found there!

Sooner or later the cry of "Has anyone seen Solo?" would start ringing round the Convent as it had done at West Stowell.

"Where's Solo?" Joan would ask Genelia, her maid.

"I haven't seen her since breakfast, my Lady." Genelia would probably reply. "She was in the small drawing-room last time I saw her."

Her earlier disappearances did not worry us much because they were in daylight, and usually ended in one of the staff announcing triumphantly, "I've got her. She was in the ......". But the day came when I foolishly declared her sensible enough to dispense with her night sand box. I had two cat flaps fitted: one out of our suite into the main corridor of the Convent, and the other in the door at the bottom of the backstairs leading into the garden. Joan felt she would never learn to find her way through the first flap, along the corridor, down the stairs, and finally negotiate the second flap into the garden, so we left the sand box in our room for a time in case Joan was proved right.

I noticed quite soon that the sand box was not being excavated as much as it used to be. Joan was also conscious that Solo was not sleeping quite as much between us either, and agreed with me that she must have mastered the obstacle course into the garden. At first she was rarely away from our bed for very long. Then one night we were woken by a vicious cat fight on the bastions of Wellington Front, the old fortifications that run between the Convent and the harbour, almost directly under our bedroom windows.

Joan was convinced that Solo had managed to scale the Convent wall and was suffering a fate worse than death at the hands of the bastion strays even though she had been neutered. Up I got and went down into the garden with a torch to try to find her. The security policeman on duty saw my torch and came to help me. There was no sign of Solo, so I went out into the road that runs between the Convent wall and Wellington Front, accompanied by the policeman. I was in my dressing gown and felt very foolish shouting "Solo, Solo, Solo ....", which degenerated at times into a string of expletives.

I dread to think what the local press would have made of the story, if someone had seen us or the policeman had talked? His Excellency, in pyjamas and dressing gown, scouring the back streets of Gibraltar, looking for his cat in the middle of the night - splendid material for some gloriously ribald headlines! I was lucky; tales of my nocturnal activity did not leak out.

Solo did not reply to my calls, and the bastion cats pushed off to fight other battles elsewhere. I went back disconsolately to confess failure to Joan, and to accept the blame for having had the cat flaps fitted in the first place. Neither of us slept much for the rest of that night, always hoping to hear the 'clonk-clonk' of the cat flap, announcing her return.

Breakfast was finished in the depths of gloom, and I went down to my office and told Tom Le Marchand that Solo had deserted. Then I started thumbing through the incoming cables, received during the night, when I heard Denise Stockdale, my W.R.A.C. secretary, call out, "Here she is! She's in our loo!" The ladies' toilet was close to Tom's office, and so it was not long before Denise handed the miscreant over to me. I went back to our suite in triumph. Holding her by the scruff of her neck in the most undignified way possible, I returned her to her mistress in disgrace.

What we had not realised so far in our short time in the Convent was that winds spring up suddenly around the Rock that can bring disaster to Governor's cats as well as seafarers. Solo, we think, had pushed her way into the downstairs ladies' loo, carrying out her self-imposed duties of disciplining the Convent mice. The wind had thoughtlessly or maliciously slammed the door behind her. Denise had found her crouching, quite unconcerned, watching one of the many crevices in the massively thick old walls where modern plumbing pipes had been tunnelled through them. She was certain that a family of mice lived there.

Solo got little sympathy from Joan for giving us such a restless night, but we had learnt lesson No. 1 in Solo safety precautions. That afternoon Joan had to open a charity bazaar. Her eyes fell on some of those sand filled door-stops, made of cloth in the shape of frogs and other creatures. Just the thing, she thought, to stop Solo being shut into rooms or being crushed by a swinging door. She returned with several, which we placed in doorways in continuous use where Solo might get herself trapped.

Lesson No. 2 occurred within a few days. Solo was missing when we wanted to go to bed.

"Oh! She'll come in when mousing is over." I said mustering enough conviction in my voice to persuade Joan not to fuss.

I did not succeed, and we were again spending another sleepless night, when at about 2 a.m. I did another of my dressing-gown patrols with the policeman around the gardens, but not, this time, in the road outside the Convent. It would have been giving some alert journalist too good an opportunity of a scoop. Solo was nowhere to be seen, so I went back to bed again feeling uncomfortably anxious. I did not believe that she could climb the garden walls, but there was a nagging doubt in my mind - perhaps she had found a low spot, or a climbable creeper growing up the wall that I not spotted during my inspections of our anti-Solo defences.

Next morning I got up early and went down into the garden as soon as it was daylight. I looked cautiously into the ladies' toilet, but found no one there. Then I opened the door into the cloisters. There was an immediate plaintive and very querulous Siamese cry coming from somewhere, but where?

I walked round looking into the various alcoves and behind historic relics, like the life-size wooden carving of General Elliott, clutching his key, but to no avail.

"No silly!" she shouted, "Up here, up here, up here! Can't you see where I'm stuck?"

I looked up and saw her small blacky-brown face sticking out from the creeper foliage at the top of one of the Cloister's pillars. She was perched on a ledge just below the windows of the upper floor of the Convent, unable to climb any higher, and yet not having the courage to scramble back down the creeper, which certainly looked very flimsy to me. Summoning Lee Gray, the gardener, who produced a ladder, I climbed up and rescued what

I hoped would be a very chastened cat. A cold night on that very narrow ledge cannot have been much fun!

Again we could only guess how Solo had managed to be in the cloisters at night anyway. I suppose she was hunting there amongst the orange trees and bougainvillea when the security policemen did their final round. She must have hidden from them, and so they did not see her when they locked up. Small birds roost on the ledge where she was trapped. She probably tried to stalk them up the creeper, but, like all cats, found the descent more difficult. That is mere speculation. We had learnt our Lesson No. 2: always check the cloisters if Solo was missing. It was one of her hunting paradises.

Lesson No. 3 was not really a lesson at all: it was a demonstration by Solo of the mysteries of the Indian rope trick, and equally baffling. The now well established routine of cat missing was triggered by her absence when we went to bed one night; garden, loos and cloisters searched; sleepless night; no cat by dawn; and then intense search by all the Convent staff. On this occasion it took rather longer to find her. I had given up and left the search to the others while we had breakfast because I was due out on an inspection of some kind at nine o'clock. It was high summer so we had it in the patio outside the Royal suite. I had just sat down when I heard that familiar voice, calling to me once more from above.

"What about me?" she seemed to be yelling, "You passed me twice last night and didn't hear me!"

"Can't you see where I am?" she yelled again, adding, "Oh! please hurry. I'm cold and hungry, and your breakfast smells delicious!"

Looking up, I saw her on the balcony outside the large drawing-room windows. How she got there we will never know. The large drawing-room had not been in use for several evenings, so it seemed unlikely that she had been shut out by one of the maids or footmen by mistake. The plumbago on the wall under the balcony had been pruned and did not reach up to it. And in any case there was quite a large overhang to be negotiated, which even an agile person like Solo would have found difficult. Rule No. 3 became check all balconies.

Rule No. 4 we soon found was watch the Convent roof. There was a staircase up onto the flat part above our suite, overlooking the south entrance of the harbour, through which most of the visiting naval task forces came when entering the Naval Base. We used to go up there quite often to watch important ships coming in, and sometimes we had coffee up there after dinner if it was stiflingly hot downstairs. The first time that we went up there was, I think, to watch a NATO force enter harbour with a number of Dutch and American as well as British ships. We did not notice that we were being followed by Solo. Instead of pulling the door onto the roof tightly shut behind me as I always did later, I left it ajar. If there is one thing, at which Solo is a dab-hand, it is opening unfastened doors of almost any size or shape. Out she came onto the roof, thrilled to have found new hunting grounds.

I saw her arrive, but did nothing about her because I was too absorbed in watching the U.S.S. *South Carolina*, one of the largest nuclear powered cruisers afloat, anchoring off the detached mole - she was too big to come inside. I had just lowered my field-glasses when I was horrified to see Solo disappearing through a very narrow gap in the tiles of the roof over the billiard room. Call as we would, she would not reply and showed no sign of returning to the surface. She was, of course, in cat heaven - mice, roaches, dead birds, spiders and every other sort of cat desirable delicacy to be found in the roof space were hers for the taking. But like most treasure troves there were difficulties in enjoying them. The snag in Solo's find was that the roof space was not solid. it contained an ornamental gallery around the ceiling of the billiard room, presumably designed to let more light onto the table before electric lights were generally available. She could not resist the temptation to jump down into the gallery, and there she got stuck.

When I arrived in the billiard room, I saw her face looking down at me once more, this time from the gallery. I could not reach her even standing on the billiard table. It was late in the evening and the gardening staff, who had the ladders locked away for security reasons, had gone home; and so I decided to be hard-hearted to teach her a lesson about always ensuring that you have a way of getting out again before venturing into attractive but dangerous places. I just looked up at her and said.

"You got in there; its up to you to get yourself out. I'll leave the roof door open. I'm sure you'll find your way out when you're hungry."

I shut the billiard-room firmly behind me and went off to have my bath and to change for dinner. I must confess that I was weak-minded enough to peep into the room again on my way down to dinner; but determined enough not to be beaten by her when I saw her face appear again through the bars of the gallery, and heard her further appeal for help. I shut the door again and continued on my way to the small drawing-room for a pre-dinner drink with Joan. She commended me for my unexpected firmness in standing up to Solo for once in my life!

I have not often won a battle of wills with Solo, but I count the battle of the billiard-room gallery as her Waterloo. After dinner we went back to our suite. There she was stuffing herself with fish as if she had never had a square meal in her life. Thereafter, we gave up fussing about her disappearances: she could look after herself - or so we thought.

CHAPTER 7

LITTLE MISS SOLIE'S ROUTINE

Soon after our arrival, I noticed that the Latin influence of the Mediterranean was changing Solo's name. I heard Genelia and the other maids calling her 'Little Miss Solie'. In my early ignorance of Gibraltarian susceptibilities, I asked Genelia if it was because 'Solo' sounded too masculine to the Spanish ear. Genelia corrected me in a trice:

"We do not have Spanish ears, Your Excellency! But Solie sounds better for a girl in Gibraltar."

I realised my *faux pas* as I said the words 'Spanish ears' instead of 'Gibraltarian ears'. 'What's the difference?' many an Anglo-Saxon would ask; and a shudder would run down every Gibraltarian spine.

"We may speak Spanish, but we are not Spanish;" said Genelia correcting me, "Everyone speaks Spanish in this part of the Mediterranean. They always have done."

Herein lies much of the Gibraltarians' difficulty in making their case to stay British. On the one hand, few people in Britain know much about their origins, and think that, because they speak Spanish rather better than English, they must be basically Spanish, which they certainly are not. And on the other, most people in Spain believe that they are renegade Spaniards, which is equally wrong. They just cannot win. The prejudices on all three sides - United Kingdom, Spanish and Gibraltarian - are just too deeply ingrained.

(It is worth noting that I have used the words 'United Kingdom' rather than 'British', because the Gibraltarians are British too, and are very proud of it. They and the Falkland

Islanders are the only former dependent peoples to be granted full British citizenship under the latest British Nationality Act.)

As I fell into the trap myself of not appreciating the true status of the Gibraltarians, I think it is worth digressing for a moment from Solo's or Solie's biography to explain who they really are.

In 1704, when Admiral Rooke took the Rock during the War of the Spanish succession, he did so *not* on behalf of Queen Anne, but for the Hapsburgs, who were claiming the Spanish throne. All but a handful of Gibraltar's Spanish inhabitants fled to the mainland, always expecting to return when the war was over and it had been decided whether the Bourbons or Hapsburgs would rule Spain. In any case, captured fortresses were usually returned to their original owners at the end of most wars in those days. Never did they expect, when peace did come with the signing of the Treaty of Utrecht in 1713, that Gibraltar would be ceded to 'Her Britannic Majesty, Queen Anne, and her heirs and successors, in perpetuity'.

Such was the enmity between Protestant Britain and Catholic Spain that the Gibraltar frontier was kept closed by Spain for almost the whole of the 18th Century. A new civilian population had to be established to help service the British naval base and garrison of the fortress. In most Western Mediterranean ports, there had always been small Genoese communities, and Gibraltar was no exception. Gibraltar's Genoese did not flee when the reputedly 'brutal' British arrived. They saw that they were onto a good thing: an empty city, labour in demand, and trade easy to come by - heaven, except for two small problems. Gibraltar was a fortress and could well come under siege again, and the city was ruled by the military: civilians had no rights.

The Genoese took such risks in their stride and summoned their relatives from Genoa to cash in on their good fortune. They provided shipwrights and sail-makers for the Royal Navy, and masons, carpenters, gardeners, other tradesmen and labourers for the garrison. Moroccan Jews arrived in small numbers to help victual the fortress despite the clause in the Treaty of Utrecht that forbade 'Jews and Moors' residing in Gibraltar - an echo of their expulsions from Spain in the 15th Century. Some Moors also came in, but most only called with their ships, carrying supplies over the Strait from North Africa, and sailed back to Morocco when they had discharged and sold their cargoes. And professional men - lawyers, bankers and merchants - arrived from England to help the military to administer the city and to profit from the Rock's potentially excellent location as a trading centre for English manufactured goods at the entrance to the Mediterranean.

Thus it came about that the new civilian population of Gibraltar, which developed in the 18th Century was largely Genoese, laced with some English genes of sailors, soldiers and professional men. The Jews kept themselves to themselves, and built up their own thriving Jewish community that exists in Gibraltar today, providing the Rock's long serving Chief Minister, Sir Joshua Hassan, who has only recently retired after forty years in office.

When Napoleon invaded Spain in 1807, Gibraltar's situation altered dramatically. Britain became the ally of the Spanish people, though not of their French dominated government. Gibraltar became one of the bases from which money, arms, clothing and supplies were run to the Spanish guerrillas, fighting Napoleon's armies. The land frontier with Spain was at last opened; Spanish girls became *persona grata* in Gibraltar; and have remained so ever since, adding Spanish blood to the original Anglo-Genoese mix.

During the Napoleonic wars, Gibraltar also became an important British naval base for Jervis's and Nelson's fleets in their struggle with the combined sea-power of France and Spain. There were often exchanges of dockyard and supply personnel between the other British naval bases of those days at Lisbon, Minorca, Leghorn, Naples, Palermo and, later, Malta, which brought Portuguese and more Western Mediterranean genes into the Gibraltarian blood stream. And, of course, there was the usual flow of seafarers, merchant adventurers, and smugglers from all over the Mediterranean to add further variety to the creation of a new people.

It took me some time and study of Government statistics, provided by that font of all knowledge on Gibraltar's history, the late Bill Cumming, the Rock's archivist, to clear my own mind about the Gibraltarians' existence. Talking to our numerous visitors about the political situation with Spain, I used to say:

"Always remember that the Gibraltarians are a people, who, though few in number - just 20,000 in Gibraltar - have lived, bred, prospered and suffered on the Rock for almost three centuries since Admiral Rooke took it in 1704."

"That is seventy-two years longer than the United States has existed since the Declaration of Independence in 1776; and just three years longer than the United Kingdom, which did not exist until the Act of Union in 1707."

"Over those three centuries, the Gibraltarians have become a people in their own right, and the Rock is their home. It is neither Britain's to give away, nor Spain's to re-acquire. In this last quarter of the 20th Century, it is the Gibraltarians' wishes, and not the provisions of some ancient treaty written in doggerel Latin - however hallowed - that must be the key to their future."

This is rather a long, but I hope worthwhile explanation of how 'Solo' became 'Solie'. Genelia was not only Joan's maid, but Solie's too; and Solie was the more demanding mistress. It was Genelia's task to sort out Solie's meals with the cooks, and to have them ready on time on the ant-proof table in Joan's bathroom with the chair set beside it. When she was off duty or had a day's leave, it was her job - certainly in Solo's view - to ensure that one of the other maids or the duty footman kept her bowl full of fresh food.

In the warm Mediterranean weather, this was like painting the Forth Bridge - a never ending task!

Solie's day began soon after midnight when she would leave our bed for what we always assumed was her anti-mouse patrol inside the Convent. The only evidence we had for this assumption was the row of tails sometimes laid out on the kitchen floor for the cooks to inspect when they arrived to cook breakfast, as if to say,

"I've enjoyed my nights work, but I don't think much of your hygiene!"

She would come back for a predawn nap on our bed, but as soon as the birds' dawn chorus began she was off on her garden patrol. She was, as ever, a great believer in the maintenance of the balance of nature, but Joan did wish that she would not involve us by bringing the victims of her culls into our bedroom - often still alive! When Joan remonstrated with her, she would look up with that pitying look in her bright blue eyes, as if to say,

"But its great fun. And you'd be overrun with sparrows, if I did not work so hard!"

Fortunately, Solie did not often catch the migrants. When she let a bird loose in our bedroom, it was, indeed, usually a sparrow, but the effect on Joan was just the same: a shriek for me or Genelia to remove the bird, which was easiest done, you would think, by throwing open the two tall double windows, overlooking the swimming-pool. The snag was that they had three layers: the inner mosquito screens, the windows themselves and the outer Spanish style shutters. All sorts of things could happen in the time it took to get those windows open, but one of two things was certain to occur: Joan would either dive under the bed clothes, if she was still in bed; or shut herself in the bathroom, if she was already up.

Although Solie had her own dining-room in Joan's bathroom, she liked to attend all our meals in case something we were having took her fancy. Breakfast was usually on the patio outside the Royal Suite. It was not a meal that she cared for much, especially if she had had a good night in the kitchen area, But, if hunting had been poor, she would demand some of the yoke of my boiled eggs on a saucer. Usually, I have two in one of those double egg-cups that look like candelabra. Losing my yoke fairly often, led to the cooks doing three boiled eggs each morning: two for me and one for Solie.

To this day, some ten years later, Solie still demands her cut of my eggs as I write her biography here at my desk at West Stowell. I always get up early to write, and eat my breakfast while I am doing so. I have learnt never to tackle my eggs until Solie has arrived to ask for her share. There would be considerable Solie umbrage, if I were to do so.

What interested her at breakfast time in the Convent more than my eggs was the arrival of Fred the tortoise, who really did like breakfast. He was very partial to a piece of buttered toast, but what he enjoyed most was a lettuce leaf and a tomato. The cooks, therefore, made the additional provision of these items to our breakfast menu, especially for Fred. Solie would watch him enjoying his repast, but, as soon as he had finished, war would be declared, and they would disappear off into the garden for their morning joust.

Lunch too was not all that popular with Solie. It did not take her long to acquire the Mediterranean habit of the afternoon siesta. After a hard morning's work in the garden, she preferred a quiet meal of fish or rabbit in Joan's bathroom before retiring for a couple of hours under a cool bush by the swimming-pool in summer, or in a soft armchair by the fire in Joan's study in winter.

Tea was quite another matter. It had echoes of the Victorian and Edwardian eras, and was very like some of the pictures of afternoon tea in the old photo albums, lying in glass cases in the drawing-room, that show life in the Convent at the turn of the century. We usually had it under the orange trees around the swimming-pool, which had not existed, of course, in those days, but the white lace table cloths and napkins, silver tea set and crumpet dish, cake stand and dainty afternoon-tea sandwiches, would have done justice to our more illustrious and leisured predecessors. Only the informality of our dress spoilt the modern picture.

Tea time was especially significant in Solie's daily routine, because there was always Marmite and toast ready for her. We had learnt about her love for Marmite during her tea with Jas Briggs in *Apollo*, and have pandered to her fad ever since.

On most days we had guests in for tea as it was an easy way to get to know people rather better than on more formal occasions, and easier still to sort out all kinds of minor, but awkward, problems like clashes between the various charities over flag-days.

The Gibraltarians are the most generous people on this earth, because they have so often suffered poverty, privation and disease in their traumatic history of sieges, epidemics and periods of economic malaise.

The problems of living through events, like the four year Great Siege near the end of the 18th Century, can easily be imagined, but few people know that the population and garrison were decimated by what was then called 'malignant fever' in the first few decades of the 19th Century. It is said to have been Yellow Fever, but could equally well have been typhus. Whatever it was, it was no respecter of persons. Rich and poor, admirals and sailors, generals and soldiers, magistrates and malefactors, patients and doctors, old and young, were all struck down with total impartiality, creating a bond between all classes in society.

After the Napoleonic Wars, Gibraltar prospered as an entrepôt centre for Mediterranean trade in British manufactured goods. The population grew rapidly, but in the 19th Century the economy boomed and slumped as it did in Victorian England, bringing serious unemployment to the over-expanded Gibraltar population. Poverty stalked the streets and malnutrition was as rife on the Rock as it was in London in Charles Dickens's time. In English cities, the rich could avoid seeing much of the poverty by living in the suburbs, but in the close confines of the fortress-city on the Rock there was no such escape. Rich and poor had to see and endure each others' company, and this experience has bred the generosity that is the hallmark of the Gibraltarians.

Joan was patron of many of the Gibraltar charities and helped most of the others, so tea was an important occasion in her day as it was for Solie, but for quite different reasons. Solie looked forward to her post-siesta snack of Marmite on toast. When the duty footman brought the tea trays, there was always a rack with two pieces of toast in it and a pot of Marmite beside it. It was my daily responsibility, as far as Solie was concerned, to butter and Marmite her toast, and to cut it into small ladylike squares before presenting it to her. If there was any delay on my part, there was a querulous 'Hurry up; hurry up' from Solie; and, if I did not react fast enough, some very sharp claws would be dug into my knees.

One day it was not the Chairwoman of the League of Hospital Friends or any other of Joan's charities that came to tea, but our old friend, Jas Briggs, who had brought *Apollo* back for a refit in the naval dockyard. I was helping Joan hand round the tea cups, and I think drop scones that day, when I felt those sharp claws and heard Solie's unmistakable demand for her share. I looked round for her toast. The Marmite pot was open with its spoon sticking out, but the toast rack was empty!

"Who's nipped the cat's toast?" I asked.

Jas almost blushed under his sun tan.

"I'm most awfully sorry; I didn't know it was Solo's. I thought that you had kindly remembered my craving for Marmite. Sorry Solo, old girl, I've had the lot!"

This grave wrong was soon put right by the arrival of more toast, but I don't think Solie ever trusted Jas again. He had been one of her girlhood idols as the swashbuckling Captain of *Apollo*. Fancy taking her Marmite: what was the Navy coming to?

But Jas had the last laugh at Solie's expense. A few days later he came to say goodbye before returning to England, and we were again having tea round by the swimming pool. Solie had her toast this time without any trouble, and Jas had his. After a good wash of satisfaction, Solie started rolling over and over, enjoying the warmth of the sun drenched flag-stones around the pool.

"Don't fall in will you, Solo!" Jas said teasingly, never expecting her to be silly enough to do so.

I am pretty sure that he did not give her a surreptitious push, though I would not have put it beyond him to have done so. There was a splash, a flurry, and a very wet and furious Solie rushed past us. Only her head was dry!

Solie, like malignant fever, was no respecter of persons. Much later, we had a visit from the Lord Chief Justice of England, the late Lord Widgery, and his wife. He was due to open the recently renovated Supreme Court building, and they were staying at the Convent in the Royal Suite. We happened to be out at some function that afternoon, so they were having tea alone by the swimming pool.

Solie arrived as usual for her tea too. Unfortunately, neither the Lord Chief Justice, nor Lady Widgery, spoke Siamese, so her case was not put down for a hearing that afternoon. After clawing Lord Widgery's trousers, she sat back and tried to hypnotize him, but the highest judicial officers of the realm do not succumb to such treatment. An impasse would have ensued had not the duty footman intervened. He understood her pleading, and whipped her up and carried her off to the kitchen for her toast. Reporting to Joan later, he said,

"Little Miss Solie wanted to have tea with the Lord Chief Justice, my Lady: I didn't think it was right'."

As Governor's cat, I suppose she was really within her rights. The Convent, after all, was as much her home as ours, certainly in her view, if in no one else's!

Dinner was a time when she exerted her rights as the Governor's cat most vigorously. The Governor - again in her view - had the greatest freedom of choice of anyone on the Rock. As his cat, so did she. Little did she know that, though she might be right in constitutional theory, this was just not so in practice. My day was timed to the minute. I was a slave to the daily programme produced by Tom Le Marchand, my Military Assistant.

My programme was the sum of all the demands on my time made by the Gibraltar Government, the Judiciary, the Service Commanders, the religious leaders - Catholic, Protestant, Jewish, Moslem and Hindu - public bodies, schools, charitable institutions, sports clubs, and 'Uncle Tom Cobbly and all!' It was timed to the minute because, as I explained when describing our arrival, Gibraltar is so small that you cannot catch up time, if you start out late for an engagement; and it is just as difficult to slip off time, if you are early.

But there had to be a bit of reserve time somewhere, and this was usually allowed for on the main staircase, leading down to the Convent's main entrance. We would leave our suite in good time, and then shed any surplus minutes by waiting on the stairs, out of sight of anyone passing in the street outside the entrance, until we had the signal from the duty footman that it was time to get into the Daimler. If we had overdone the time reserve and were much too early, or there was some hitch like a traffic jam to delay our departure, Joan would sit down on one of the stairs, quietly reciting A.A. Milne's Christopher Robin ditty:

"This is the stair where I always sit;

There isn't any other stair quite like it;

It's not at the bottom;

It's not at the top;

This is the stair where I always stop!"

Solie, of course, knew none of this. She had no staff to restrict her freedom of choice, which she liked to exercise to the full at dinner time. The first decision was whether to have supper at the table in Joan's bathroom, or wait to have dinner with us in the dining-room. On most evenings her tummy won the argument and she opted for early supper. But, if she had been out to the kitchen and found that we were to have one of her favourite dishes, like swordfish steak grilled in butter, she would spruce herself up as we changed for dinner, and accompany us to the small drawing-room for our pre-dinner aperitif.

Once in the small drawing-room, she could exercise her right of choice again. Where should she sit for maximum comfort and enjoyment? Any reasonable cat would have sat herself down in front of the log fire, if it was winter time, to enjoy its warmth; or on the balcony, if it was summer time, to enjoy the breeze. Not so Solie: Spring, Summer, Autumn, Winter, she had to have a lap. It would have been reasonable if she had chosen Joan's. She was after all Joan's cat, and most of Joan's evening dresses were patterned and would not have shown the grey hairs that she left on her chosen lap. She would invariably go for mine or the A.D.C.'s black dinner-jacket trousers. Poor Sergeant Andrews, my batman, and Private Cummings, the A.D.C.'s, had to spend hours brushing our trousers down next morning, and had clothes-brushes full of Siamese fur.

When dinner was announced, and the tall double doors of the

dining-room were opened, Solo was always the first to react, forgetting that I, as Her Majesty's Representative in Gibraltar, should lead the way into dinner. Fortunately her slavish adherence to her anti-terrorist drills prevented any breach of protocol. She would take her usual zigzag course from one piece of furniture to the next, and allow me ample time to overtake her!

Solie's ultimate choice came once she was in the dining-room. Should she sample the first course or wait patiently for the second and main course? Unlike any ordinary cat, the Governor's cat was prepared to sit demurely behind my chair until the course that she had chosen during her evening visit to the kitchen was served. Knowing her preferences, I would cut up a piece of whatever I judged was Solie-attractive and handed it down to her on a saucer specially provided for the purpose. Sometimes she was just too polite, or I was regrettably forgetful and did not give her what she felt was her due before the steward cleared the course away. In the most expressive Siamese that she could muster, she would tell me what she thought of me:

"What about me?"

"I've waited patiently and politely - what's the use?"

A claw or two into my leg would make the point. The trouble was that, by that time, I had eaten my share, and so had Joan and the A.D.C. All I could do was to make soothing noises, telling her that she would not have liked the course anyway. I would pick her up at the end of the meal and take her to Joan's bathroom, while coffee was being served, and suggest to her that her original supper was far more tasty. It never worked. She just chalked up another black mark against me, muttering something about what a mistake she had made to think that I was her friend!

Bed-time, like dinner-time, was decision time too. Should she come to bed with us or go hunting? We made no attempt to influence her choice. Usually she chose the first quarter of the night to hunt for mice in the kitchen area; the second quarter was spent curled up between us; the third, just before dawn, she used to ensure that everyone was getting up in the garden; and for the last quarter she was back in bed with us, sleeping off her night's

93

exertions, the success of which could be judged by the number of mouse tails laid out as scalps in the kitchen.

And so back to the beginning of the daily cycle once more.

CHAPTER 8

THE QUEEN'S BIRTHDAY

Within four days of our arrival on the Rock, we were thrown willy-nilly into the Queen's Birthday celebrations, in which, I as her Majesty's Representative in Gibraltar, had to play the principal, if untutored, role. There was the Queen's Birthday parade by the resident battalion in the morning; then the naval steam-past and R.A.F. fly-past in the afternoon; and finally, the traditional Garden Party at the Convent in the evening.

Joan, I, and Solo (she had not yet become Solie) were complete novices in such important ceremonial. Solo seemed to sense our apprehension, and decided to be as helpful as she could. She appreciated that, as Governor's cat, she had certain responsibilities of her own in keeping up appearances. It would never do for her to let us down in any way on such a very public occasion. Indeed, she was determined to add dignity to the events by emulating the Queen's 'Beasts' in her own deportment. Her principal position would be sitting very upright and very still, as they did, in some prominent place so that all our guests would see her, and comment on her grace and elegance!

The Queen's Birthday parade, which is a replica of Trooping the Colour on Horse Guards in London, takes place on the Naval No 1 Sports Ground that lies close to the centre of the city. Though used for cricket, football and hockey, it has a hard gravel surface suitable for ceremonial parades. Grass would not survive the Mediterranean heat and the shortage of water in summer. It is also nicely overlooked by the Line Wall - the original seaward defence of Gibraltar - from which those who do not obtain a seat in the stands erected on the ground itself, can watch the parade.

The dress for the parade, as in London, is full-dress for those taking part and Ascot-style rig for the invited spectators in the stands. One of the features of life in Gibraltar that impressed me most was the wish of all Gibraltarians to stay British, and be able to show their loyalty to Her Majesty by behaving even better than Her subjects in the United Kingdom. One of the symbols of Britain's determination to respect the wishes of the Gibraltarians is the continuance of the pomp and ceremony of the Imperial era. Even Solo changed from her everyday blue collar, which matched her eyes, to a scarlet one for the Queen's Birthday.

Dressing for major ceremonial events was always an intricate business for me and Sergeant Andrews, which Solo enjoyed and always tried to help. My outfit for the parade was the same white summer uniform jacket and red-striped blue 'overall' trousers that I had worn on our arrival in *Apollo*. When I had got dressed in *Apollo*, Solo had been fighting back the effects of the tranquillizer that I had given her for disembarkation, so she had not been able to show any interest in what was going on around her. This time she was wide-eyed with interest. There were so many cat-attractive things laid out for her to inspect.

The gold tassels of my waist sash were the first items to catch her attention. They needed, in her view, sorting out just as thoroughly as the pencils on my desk at West Stowell. The only trouble was that they would not roll onto the floor as pencils did. In her annoyance she gave a big enough tug for the whole sash to slip off the chair and engulf her. There was no harm done except to her dignity.

"That'll teach her!" Sergeant Andrews sighed and recovered it from her.

She next had to examine my three knight's stars, medals and British Empire sash on my tunic hanging over the back of a chair ready for Sergeant Andrews to help me into it. There was again no harm in this, but he took the precaution of returning it to its hanger and suspending it well out of her reach on a hook on the back of the door.

Then her attention was attracted by my spurs, which jingled as

I walked round the dressing-room. Why did they jingle? She just had to find out!

Her first method of doing so was to lie on her side and to kick them vigorously with her back paws as cats do when playing with a mouse or soft joy. Again no harm was done.

Then she tried pawing them from the standing position with the inevitable result. She rubbed up against my trouser legs. Poor Sergeant Andrews almost had a fit. Hours of careful brushing of the navy blue serge to ensure that not a speck of fluff would mar my appearance, had been ruined in a flash. A band of grey and white Siamese fur appeared around my legs at about a foot from the ground!

Solo was immediately banished, and, thereafter, was forbidden the freedom of my dressing-room whenever ceremonial dress was the order of the day. She was most offended. To make amends on that occasion, I suggested that she should see the parade on the television set in the small drawing-room with the staff. She condescended to do so, and stayed with them almost to the end of the parade, when, as I will describe later, she left in rather a hurry.

The Queen's Birthday Parade in Gibraltar is naturally on a smaller scale than Trooping the Colour on Horse Guards Parade, but it lacks nothing in poignancy. In many ways it pulls more at the heart strings, because of the ever-present Spanish challenge to Her Majesty's sovereignty over the Rock. In my days as Governor, that challenge was symbolised by the hermetically sealed frontier and the absence of ferries across the Bay to Algeciras. Even though the frontier is now open, the challenge has not lessened. Only the Spanish tactics have changed to what the Gibraltarians aptly describe as osmosis - the gradual infiltration of Spanish influence, economic interest, and culture so that one day they may be able to take-over. As I will be describing later, they are going about it in a curiously inept way.

The parade begins as the Governor and his wife step out of the Daimler at the saluting base. As the car drives off and he mounts the dais, the order for the Royal Salute rings out. The rifles of the white jacketed and blue trousered ranks of the resident battalion - 2nd Queen's Regiment during our first year - shimmer as they present arms - and the first three bars of the National Anthem ring out for the first of six times that day. Then the high-pitched trills of fife and drum can be heard as the Escort to the Keys, provided by the Gibraltar Regiment, marches onto the parade ground, with the white helmeted Port Sergeant at their head, carrying the Keys. They halt in front of the Governor, and the Port Sergeant salutes. With a rattle, which is audible even on the Line Wall above the parade ground, he thrusts the Keys out at arms length and the Governor takes them with a flourish and equally loud rattle.

I have mentioned already that General Sir George Elliott, the victorious defender of Gibraltar against the combined might of France and Spain in the Great Siege of 1878-82, always carried the keys of the fortress at his belt and slept with them at night. The reason for this was simple: anti-treachery. Political disaffection, bribery and subversion are not 20th Century inventions. Throughout history, more fortresses have fallen through internal disloyalty than external assault. Fortress commanders could never be too careful!

In the 18th Century, there were only three practical ways of getting into Gibraltar: by landing from the sea, but the Royal Navy stood in the way; by blowing a breach in the immensely strong northern defences, but the Royal Artillery and the Royal Engineers were able to prevent that happening; or by bribing someone inside the city to open the Land Port, the only gate that the Spanish infantry could possibly reach over land. Elliot was well aware of the danger, and would never allow the Keys out of his sight, except when the Port Sergeant had to open the Land Port at dusk each evening for the outpost company to take up its alarm positions outside the fortress for the night; and at dawn when they came back in again.

The Keys have become not only the symbol of the Rock's impregnability, but also of its British Sovereignty. The Governor no longer takes them to bed with him, but they always lie on a silken cushion in front of him at all meals in the Convent dining-room. The colour of the cushion changes with the Service of the Governor: scarlet for a general, dark blue for an admiral, and light blue for an air marshal.

My predecessors used to carry the Keys, dangling them at their sides from the great iron ring, during all ceremonial occasions. I made one significant change in my determination to enhance Gibraltar's identity. I started saluting with the Keys as a field marshal would use his baton. The change was greeted with approval by the Gibraltarians, but sometimes I regretted it: holding half a stone of wrought iron aloft while a battalion marches past takes a modicum of willpower! My successor, Admiral Sir David Williams, carried on doing so; but I hear that they are now laid on their cushion on a table beside the Governor during parades.

After the Port Sergeant has handed over the Keys, the parade goes ahead as if it was taking place on Horse Guards Parade. The Governor inspects the battalion: the Queen's Colour is trooped; the battalion marches past in slow and quick time; but then comes an important difference. As soon as the battalion is ready to advance in review order to pay their final complements to their Sovereign, the Governor steps down from the dais and takes up his position in front of the Colonel on the parade ground. The Royal Standard is broken over the dais, symbolising the arrival of her Majesty to take the final salute.

On the Colonel's word of command, the long white and blue ranks of the battalion advance fifteen paces in line, halt and present arms. For the second time, the National Anthem rings out, but this time it is complete and not just the three bars to which the Governor is entitled. The Gibraltar Regiment saluting battery at Devil's Gap above the city starts a twenty-one gun salute. As the noise of the last round dies away the Colonel orders 'hats off' and the Governor leads the three cheers for Her Majesty. The National Anthem sounds again for the third time, and the parade presents arms as the Royal Standard is lowered. The Queen has left.

The Governor returns to the dais and re-assumes his real-life status as Her Majesty's Representative. He receives his own farewell Royal Salute - the fourth of the day - before the Daimler pulls up in front of him. The A.D.C. escorts the Governor's wife from the spectators' stand to join him in the car and they drive back to the Convent together.

I must admit that, on this first occasion, I felt an enormous sense of relief as we reached the haven of the Convent. No great disaster had occurred. I had not dropped the Keys; I had not tripped over my spurs mounting and stepping down from the dais; and above all, I had got the timing of the three cheers for Her Majesty right. I had not given a word of command on a ceremonial parade since I left the Queen's Gurkha Engineers in Malaya in 1960! I was far from sure that my voice would carry. However, adrenalin had surged and all was well!

When we arrived back in our suite to change out of our finery for lunch Solo was nowhere to be found. Genelia reported that she had left the small drawing-room in panic when the Gibraltar Regiment's gun had started firing the Royal Salute. She had looked high and low for her without success. I ordered a full scale cat search at once, but that achieved nothing. The Colonel and his principal officers on the parade were expected with their wives at any moment, so I called off the search and we went out into the garden to give them a thank-you drink for all the hard work that they had put into making the parade a success.

Joan was desperately worried, so the drinks party degenerated into a disguised Solo hunt. She and I took our guests around the gardens, drinks in hand, theoretically to admire Lee and Carol Gray's gardening skill. They had brought the closely packed flower-beds to their peak of perfection for the Garden Party that evening. Solo could have been anywhere in those carpets of colour. We saw Fred ruminating under some large shady lilies, but there was no sign of Solo.

It was not until after lunch that Solo emerged. I suppose we should have remembered her first days at West Stowell and her instinctive tactical flare for finding a defensive position from which she could see without being seen. We should also have been suspicious of any cupboard door that was slightly ajar. Joan went to put her hat away in its box in the bottom of one of her wardrobes. It wasn't empty. Two bright blue eyes set in a black face were staring up at her!

Solo emerged looking cross. I think from the tone of her voice she was complaining about those dreadful gunners at Devil's Gap. Would I, as Governor, kindly order the salute to be fired from elsewhere? Needless to say her request was not even considered, though the guns were subsequently moved for quite different reasons to the parade ground itself so that the Gibraltar Regiment Gunners could play a more prominent part in the parade. Until that happened in our last year in Gibraltar, she just had to get used to salutes, which, as the days went by, we began to realise were pretty frequent occurrences.

As well as salutes being fired to mark special days in the Calendar, like St George's Day or Prince Philip's or the Queen Mother's Birthdays, the salutes of visiting British and Allied warships had to be returned. Solo never got use to them, but we did not worry to look for her. She would re-emerge when she was sure that her Gunner enemies had had their fun for the day at her expense.

Solo could not even see, let alone play any part in the afternoon's naval display because there is no good view of the Bay from the Convent, which is low down behind the bastions. Naval concentrations at Gibraltar do not always coincide with the Queen's Birthday, but in 1978 there were nine British, Canadian and American submarines returning to harbour after a NATO exercise. Admiral Michael Stacey, who was Flag Officer, Gibraltar when we arrived, kindly suggested that I should fly my Governor's flag in the guard-ship, H.M.S. *Aurora*, and take their salute as they entered the Bay.

There was a slight sea mist in the Strait with the mountains of Morocco rising above it, which provided an awe-inspiring back-drop to the event. As I stood on top of *Aurora*'s bridge ready to take the salute, the submarines loomed out of the mist, a sinister line of Leviathan like black whales climbing out of Hades. It was an unforgettable occasion, which I never had the privilege to enjoy again. The following year there was a concentration of surface ships in harbour, but unfortunately a thick sea fog blanketed the Strait and put paid to any steam-past. Regrettably, no other naval concentrations during our time coincided with the Queen's Birthday, which was a pity.

As the last submarine passed *Aurora*, six R.A.F. jets from North Front flew low up the Bay in their Queen's Birthday tribute, turning sharply round the north end of the Rock to avoid infringing Spanish airspace. One of the many irritants imposed on Gibraltar by Spain was the strict enforcement of her air boundaries. Aircraft landing at North Front had to do a ninety degree turn at the head of the Bay just before touching down on the runway, despite all the risks that this posed to both civilian passenger and military aircraft, particularly in bad weather when the Rock itself is causing air turbulence on the approach.

Solo made up for her dislike of the Gunners and disdain for submarines and aircraft by thoroughly enjoying the Garden Party in the evening. 'Garden Party' is a misnomer. There are no Victorian tea urns, cups and saucers, and plates of dainty sandwiches and iced cakes. The party starts at six, with alcohol in all its many guises rather than tea providing the social stimulant, and in consequence is much more enjoyable and goes far better. Seven hundred guests are invited and certainly come, if they possibly can, because it is the main social function of the year. The gardens are at their best, everyone wants to be seen, and the drinks are free. The Governor pays!

The main topic of conversation at our first Garden Party was how difficult it must be for us to host such a party so soon after our arrival. We could but agree while at the same time giving the credit to the staff, and particularly to Sergeant Feeney, for organising it so splendidly for us. Being thrown in it so early in our time on the Rock had one great advantage and one not so happy disadvantage as we found out later. The advantage was easy to see. Although we knew very few of our guests, they could all meet us and make up their minds whether they liked the new Governor and his wife or not. We became part of the Gibraltar

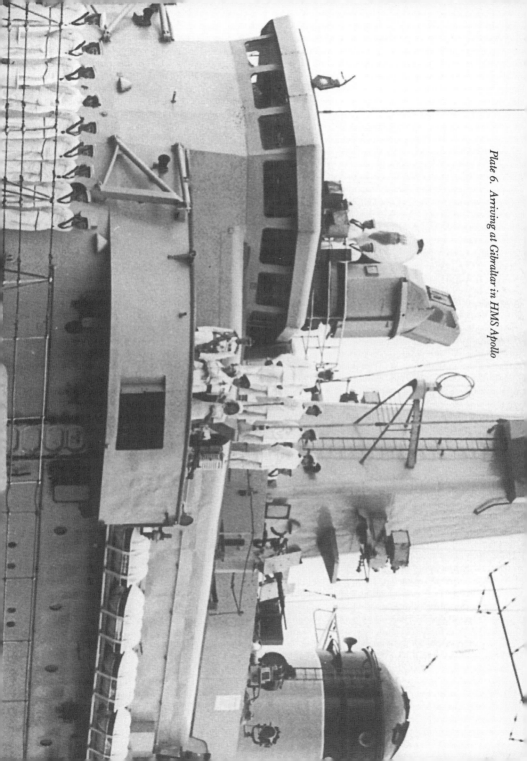

Plate 6. Arriving at Gibraltar in HMS Apollo

Above: Plate 7. Gibraltar seen from my fishing ground off Europa point with the Governor's Barge in the foreground. The Governor's Cottage is three-quarters of the way up the nearest peak. Below: Plate 8. The Convent entrance (left) with the east end of King's Chapel (right). (Paintings by Vin Mifsud)

Plate 9. The Napier Wing with our suite on the top floor and the Royal Suite below One of Solo's favourite spots was the balcony outside our suite.

Above: Plate 10. *The original part of the Convent seen from the garden*
Below: Plate 11. *The Dining-room. (Paintings by Vin Mifsud)*

Above: Plate 12. The Cloisters, where Solo used to get trapped climbing the crepers after the birds. Below: Plate 13. The Governor's Cottage. (Paintings by Vin Mifsud)

Above: Plate 14. The patio fountain, one of Solo's favourite spots. (Paintinf by Vin Mifsud).
Below: Plate 15. Solo's mistress with the Rock Apes

Plate 16. The Staff at the Convent. Back Row: Mr Oulkadi, Mr Saliva, Mr Dalmedo, Mr Ezzareg, Mr Ezzidi, Mrs Stewart, Pte Coghlan, Cpl Brennan, L/Cpl Reeves, Sgt Andrews. Second Row: Mrs Pitia, Mrs Sisarello, Mrs Asquez, Mrs Perea, Mrs Finlayson, Mr Finlayson, Cpl Crockett, Cpl Crockett (WRAC), S/Sgt Davies (WRAC), Sgt Hudson (WRAC), Sgt Sanchez, L/Cpl Philips, L/Cpl Headrick, Sgt Briggs, Sgt Feeney, L/Cpl Phenny. Front Row: FCPO Partington, Capt Sexton, Lady Jackson, the author, Lt Col Thomson, Miss Peters

Above: Plate 17. Solo in the drawing-room with her mistress and master.
Below: Plate 18. Our farewell photograph.

social scene for better or worse very quickly and painlessly! What we did not realise was how many people would expect us to recognise them afterwards on the strength of a fleeting meeting that evening.

Joan wondered what to do about Solo. Should she lock her in our bedroom in case she took fright at the sight of so many people? We decided that it would be the best thing to do, but, when we came to look for her, she had done one of her vanishing tricks. She could thought read as well as most animals, and she was not going to be shut up. She was going to enjoy the party, and she did!

The first time that I noticed that she had emerged from hiding was while we were shaking hands with our guests as they arrived in the garden before being wafted off by the Honorary ADCs to one of the four bars set up in the gardens to select the drink of their choice. She was sitting discreetly hidden by the trunk of the large palm tree planted by Kaiser Wilhelm II during his visit to the Rock in 1906. No-one seemed to notice her. She was having a gorgeous time appraising the cat-attractiveness of various guests. One thing that Siamese are particularly bad at, and Solo was no exception, is deciding who likes cats and who does not. She only looked at people through her own eyes without a thought for her potential friend or victim's feelings. If she liked the look of someone, she could not conceive that that person might dislike her. Disasters often occurred by her insisting on rubbing herself up against some cat disliker's legs with the consequential distress to both parties: neurotic shuddering by the victim and hurt feelings for Solo! So far so good; as long as she stayed behind Kaiser Bill's palm tree, all would be well.

One of the hazards that we had not anticipated before the party started was the effect of shaking some seven hundred hands. Fortunately I wear only a signet-ring on my left hand and nothing on the right. Poor Joan wanted to look her best and had rings on both hands. By the time she had shaken the seven hundredth hand, the rings on her right hand had bitten into her fingers and had drawn blood! It was a lesson for future garden parties.

I mentioned the Honorary ADCS. There were three of them. The most senior was Commander Joe Ballantine of the Gibraltar unit of the Royal Naval Reserve, H.M.S. *Calpe.* He was a veteran of many Garden Parties, and knew everything there was to know about them except how to treat a Siamese cat under such circumstances. The second was Captain Arthur Michael Rugeroni of the Gibraltar Regiment, who was also a Garden Party warrior without Siamese experience. And the third was Inspector Charles Colombo of the Gibraltar Police, who was new to both Garden Parties and Siamese! Joe took Joan round the guests in a clockwise direction, introducing her to as many people as possible, while Arthur Michael helped me as we went round in the opposite direction. Charles Colombo and Andy Craig, our regular ADC, were free to deal with the many minor crises that occur on such occasions. It was Solo, however, who took her duties most seriously of all. She came over to me as I started out with Arthur Michael on my circuit of the guests to act as the party 'ice-breaker'.

I was not immediately conscious of her offer of assistance. The first I knew of it was a gentle brush against my leg. Looking down, I saw Solo rubbing around my trousers in an affectionate way, as if saying 'Introduce me too'. I bent down, picked her up and did just that. She was graciously pleased to allow the guests, to whom I happened to be talking, to stroke her head and admire her brilliant blue eyes that shone all the bluer in the mellow evening sunlight. She was charming to everyone, and even condescended to purr. The main topic of conversation, as I moved from group to group, was her age, sex and type - seal point, lilac point, or blue point - and, of course, her secret arrival in *Apollo.* She was enjoying being the centre of attraction and showing herself off in the security of my arms as the Governor's very own cat when I felt her stiffen suddenly and decide that she could stay no longer.

'Really, I do think it is the limit' she said, squirming around, trying to jump out of my arms. 'How could you invite such people. I can't stay a moment longer. I'm off!'

And she was. A few zigzag turns between the guests and she went leaping like a small gazelle across the lawns to the safety of the Convent.

Who it was that offended her we will never know. It could have been some cat-discordant note played by the band of the resident battalion, which was providing discreet background music. Or it could have been the jangling of a charm bracelet as a female guest stretched out an arm to stroke her.

Whatever it was put an end to Solo's enjoyment of her first major Convent function as Governor's Cat. She, like Joan and I, was now known to Gibraltarian society - for better or worse!

It is wrong to apply the words 'Gibraltarian society' to the guests at our first Garden Party. Joan and I found that the guest list was only about a third Gibraltarian to two thirds expatriate Britons - government officials, professional people, senior management of banks and commercial firms, officers of all three Services and, incidentally, almost all the naval nursing sisters. We both felt that this was wrong, but we could do nothing about it on that occasion because the invitations had been sent out before we arrived. Over our four and a half years on the Rock we reversed the balance gradually to two thirds Gibraltarian to one third expatriates to reinforce my efforts to make the Rock more Gibraltarian. I was far from popular amongst the Services for making this change, but I am sure it was appreciated by the Gibraltarians.

The end of the Garden Party came exactly at eight o'clock. With meticulous timing the ADCs managed affairs so that Joan and I met in front of the Convent patio on the completion of our clockwise and anti-clockwise circuits just as the band was ready to play the National Anthem for the sixth time that day. There was the customary roll of drums as the 'Queen' brought the day that Joan, I and Solo will always remember.

As we walked back into the Convent we found Solo watching the guests' departure from the safety of the back staircase.

As I picked her up, she gave a purr. I suspect she said:

'Thank God that's over!'

Or it may have been an apology for her rude behaviour.

Whatever she may have said did not matter very much. All three of us were delighted to be back in the privacy of our own rooms. The most hectic day of our lives was over. Solo realised this first and curled up on Joan's lap with a purr more like the rumble of a boiling kettle than an expression of pleasure of a small Siamese princess!

CHAPTER 9

LUNCHES AND DINNERS

Solo, or Solie as she became in Gibraltar, was not as gregarious as her performance at the Garden Party might suggest. She was very much our personal cat, who, willy-nilly, had to put up with all the comings and goings of the Convent staff and visitors. She had the sense of occasion befitting the Governor's Cat, but her instinct was to avoid the often noisy daily routine of the Convent, such as the cleaning women chattering at the tops of their voices over the noise of the Hoovers. She would make herself scarce by disappearing into one of her many secret hide-aways in the gardens or into her favourite wardrobe in our bedroom where there was a small, low powered electric heater to stop Joan's clothes going mildewed in the humid atmosphere of the Rock.

Joan had found Solo's wardrobe hiding-place quite early on, and had put her old cat basket in there with its original soft cushion and cast-off cardigan that she had had since she was a kitten. Giving her a boudoir of her own had the merit of providing a likely spot where she could usually be found if something had upset her.

But Solie had that second instinct, which conflicted with her desire for privacy: curiosity. Shyness and the need to investigate everything that caught her attention fought a tug of war in her small mind every time there was a lunch or dinner party in the Convent, which was all too frequent. We found that former ADCs had divided society in Gibraltar into four categories: those who were invited to dinner; to lunch; to cocktail parties; and, at the bottom of the list, those who came only to the Garden Party. Joan and I never liked large cocktail parties: they were too impersonal, far too noisy, and generally not worth the time and effort of laying them on. If we wanted to get to know people properly - and we did - we felt lunch or supper parties, usually in the informality of the garden patio when the weather allowed, were the best way of doing so. Dinner parties held in the vast dining-room were too formal, and were reserved for high-level visitors and special occasions.

When we were by ourselves and the weather was anything between warm and sweltering, we had most of our meals in the garden patio, which was outside the Royal suite. In the centre there was a two tier circular fountain. The upper tier acted as an over large drinking bowl for sparrows and bathing pool for blackbirds; and the lower, at ground level and very much larger and deeper, was filled with gold fish of all shapes and sizes that bred and inter-bred prolifically amongst the lilies and water plants. Unfortunately, Mohammed, the Moroccan handyman, who was responsible for the cleanliness of the patio amongst his many other duties, had introduced one or two grey looking non-goldfish, and so some of the progeny were distinctly piebald: some red, some silver, some black and some a combination of all three in differing patterns!

The fountain was Solie's pride and joy. It served her in two ways. First, she loved to watch the birds on the rim of the upper bowl, which she could not reach without falling into the lower bowl. She would sit for hours growling, gnashing her teeth and sometimes swearing loudly at them in her frustration at not being able to help herself to a meal of fresh bird. She also liked to dream of an even more succulent repast of fresh goldfish, but they were too quick for her and she did not like getting her paws wet anyway! Surprisingly she never fell in as far as we know. She was sure that the fountain's main purpose was for *her* entertainment.

Its secondary purpose in her view was to provide a way of viewing our lunch party guests without committing herself to joining them during prelunch drinks on the lawns. There were four well stocked and colourful flower-beds around the fountain through which she could creep ostensibly to discipline the birds and goldfish. If she liked the look of the company, she would emerge and sit demurely on the path, expecting some cat-lover to notice her sooner or later. If sooner, her courage might fail her and she would withdraw precipitately back into the cover of the flower-beds with an appropriate display of female coyness. If it was later and she had had time to examine the guests for some time, she might roll over on her side, which was her way of saying 'Do pick me up; I'd love to talk to you'. Any guest so invited felt truly honoured because I would assure him or her that this was a most unusual sign of affection - which was true up to a point.

After a time, however, Solie decided that it was incumbent upon her as Governor's Cat to play her full part at lunch parties as assistant hostess to Joan. Having viewed the guests from afar, she would select the most cat-attractive and walk delicately towards her choice to give his or her leg a gentle brush with her sleek fur coat. She then became the centre of attraction and softened any tendency to awkwardness in the prelunch conversation. Even the shyest of guests found something to talk about in her presence. But there was one remark Solie could not stand and that was 'I do love Siamese; they're more like dogs than cats'. Deeply offended at any reference to those, to her, beastly anti-cat animals was just too much. Out would come her claws as she struggled free from her admirer's arms and she would dash off in high dudgeon at such an insult!

During our first few months on the Rock, I paid a visit to a different Government department each Thursday to meet the staff and to learn something of their problems at first hand. It might be the Electricity Department one week, the Postal Service the next, Water the week after ... and so on. After each visit the minister responsible for the department and its director would come to lunch at the Convent with their wives. When I had completed my initial visits to all departments, Joan and I visited a different school each week and by the end had talked to the children in almost every classroom in Gibraltar! The head and assistant head of each school with their spouses came to lunch at the end of each visit too. And then there were the visiting naval and air squadrons of all the NATO nations whose commanders came to lunch if there was no dinner party that particular week; and, of course, there were many other miscellaneous visitors, who had to be entertained in one way or another. It all added up to about two lunch parties a week.

Solie never missed a lunch party or any other function for that matter, but she was pretty choosy about which she actually joined. On one occasion, her judgment of human frailties let her and us down very badly. Joan was hosting a special lunch party for wives of senior members of the Bar at the opening of the Legal Year, while I was attending the actual Bar luncheon at the Rock Hotel. Suddenly one of the most senior guests went pale, rigid, and barely able to speak. She could only point to one of the flower-beds. Solie was just emerging to approach her selected guest, quite unaware that her choice was desperately allergic to cats and especially Siamese!

That meant a warning to all ADCs. They always checked guest lists to see whether anyone coming to a meal at the Convent had special religious scruples or medical problems that made certain dishes inappropriate (for Jews, no shell fish and only Kosher meat; for Moslems, no pork; for Hindus, no beef; for Catholics, only fish on Fridays, and so on), but they now had to check for Siamese allergy problems as well.

Unfortunately, the lady first shocked by Solie was a frequent guest, so Solie had to be locked firmly away in Joan's bedroom whenever she came to the Convent. Solie never understood why and was always indignant about her incarceration.

Dinners were always very formal occasions and occurred, once, twice or sometimes three times a month in busy seasons, which tended to coincide with major NATO exercises and Parliamentary recesses, when not only ministers of the Crown could get away from Westminster, but high-ranking officials - civilian and military - could leave their desks in Whitehall as Parliamentary questions did not have to be answered. January was the most active month: both the Christmas recess and winter weather coincided to prompt official visits to warmer climes, sometimes on the thinnest of excuses!

Despite being in the Mediterranean, we could never guarantee good weather at that time of year, because the Rock lies in a wind tunnel between Europe and Africa, and manufactures its own climate in most unpredictable ways. January was one of the least dependable months, but at least we could claim that it would be warmer than London. Though we might see snow on the Sierra Nevadas in Spain to the north and on the Atlas Mountains to the south, it rarely, if ever, snows in Gibraltar and frost is virtually unknown. Nevertheless, there can be deluges of rain and biting winds. There was no central heating in the Convent, and all the windows and doors generated drafts as they were designed to do in summer. During cold spells we kept the place reasonably warm with large log fires that burned old tar-impregnated wood stripped out of warships during refits in the Dockyard; and protected ourselves with thick winter woollies.

Our prospective guests never seemed to be deterred by our doubts about the weather. 'Oh! Gib's in the Med.' they would say, 'It can't be worse than London!' After a winter Levanter had been blowing for several weeks and a dozen inches of rain had fallen in as many days, we admired their confidence.

I must digress for a moment to say something about Gibraltar's curse: the Levanter. We and everyone else in Gibraltar would become crotchety and bad tempered when it was blowing. Even Solie disliked it and went off her food. It is the east wind, which blows off the Mediterranean and forms the characteristic white cloud that streams off the top of the Rock like the plume of a Horse Guardsman's helmet in a strong wind. It is picturesque for those living in nearby Spain and for passengers on passing ships, but far from attractive for those living on the Rock under its dampening influence.

The Levanter is caused by the wind blowing across the hot Mediterranean, which acts like a huge pan of boiling water, super-saturating the air as it passes over it. When the wind hits the steep, 1,300 foot, back of the Rock, it is forced upwards, cooling swiftly and condensing into steamy cloud as it rises. It then topples down into the city (and the Convent) on the other side. Everything becomes damp in the high humidity; the warm sun is shut out; and lethargy takes over with all the accompanying human ailments associated with damp climates. The ever-present

'Mañana' or 'Tomorrow' syndrome of the Mediterranean is reinforced: things just do not get done during the Levanter.

There is the hackneyed Spanish joke about Gibraltar:

'Why is Gibraltar British?'

'Because it attracts English weather!'

A further digression may interest readers not familiar with Gibraltar, although it has nothing to do with Solie. Water has always been a problem. In earlier times, when the population was a third of what it is today, it was just possible to catch enough rain water from the run-offs from roofs, which was stored in tanks under the houses, to eke out the limited amount available from wells. In the Victorian era, the ingenuity of Sapper officers led to the sinking of wells in the isthmus between the Rock and Spain, which provided undrinkable, brackish water. Two systems of water supply were established: fresh water for drinking and cooking, and brackish for all other purposes.

At the beginning of this century, Anglo-German naval rivalry led to the construction of the great torpedo-proof naval base for the British Atlantic and Mediterranean fleets. The military and civilian populations grew rapidly, and so did the demand for water. Again Sapper ingenuity came to the rescue. The back of the Rock forms an ideal water-catchment area. In prehistoric times, when the Mediterranean was a desert basin, sand was blown up against the Rock by its hot swirling winds, forming a natural slope of tightly packed, wind blown sand that the Sappers saw could serve as the foundation for a roof-like water run-off. Today, as you look at the East face of the Rock from the sea, it seems as though the great sand slope has been covered with concrete to form the catchment, but this is not so.

When I took guests on a Rock tour and we reached O'Hara's Battery, perched on the most southerly peak of the Rock, and with magnificent all-round views, I used to give them three guesses as to what the catchment was made out of. Only those with some prior knowledge ever guessed right. It is a vast expanse of corrugated iron sheeting! Concrete slabs would have been too heavy to fix firmly onto that steep, unstable bank of prehistoric sand. The solution adopted was to drive rows of timber stakes into it, and then lay horizontal wooden joists across them to form a framework onto which the metal sheets could be securely nailed. The finished job looks like one side of a giant corrugated iron roof some 800 feet high. The rain hits the sheeting and runs down the corrugations into concrete lined channels that carry it into underground storage tanks dug deep inside the Rock.

The water tanks themselves are well worth a visit too. They are like enormous coffins cut in the limestone. Each is about a hundred feet long and perhaps thirty feet wide and deep. They are laid out in serried ranks down a large vaulted tunnel. Water vapour rises from them constantly, which, in the eerie glow of the dim electric lighting, makes them look a way up from Hades from which the dead could emerge for the last count on the Day of Judgment!

Even the construction of the catchment area and the underground storage tanks could not satisfy the demand for water by the growing population. In our day, there were six sea water distillation plants - three civil and three military - producing fresh water, and two small tankers bringing water over from Morocco. Water is never taken from Spain because Gibraltar could not take the political risk of becoming dependent upon Spanish supplies for this vital commodity. In unusually dry years, recourse has to be made to shipping very expensive tanker loads of water from Northumbria.

You may be wondering how and when the Mediterranean came to be a desert from which the hot sand was driven by fierce winds up onto the back of the Rock. One explanation is that several ice-ages ago Europe and Africa were joined by a hilly isthmus where the Straits are today. The Mediterranean was an arid basin lying several hundred feet below the Atlantic's water level with several large saline lakes in it, surrounded by desert, very much like the Dead Sea today. When the ice melted after one particular ice age, the water level of the Atlantic rose sufficiently high for the tides to batter their way through the isthmus into the lower Mediterranean basin. When the breakthrough occurred, the rush of Atlantic water was so great that it gouged out the 3,000 foot deep trench in the sea bed that can be seen on models and maps of the Straits of Gibraltar today.

The ancient Greeks seem to have had some idea of what happened as they attributed the formation of the Straits to the Labours of Hercules. They imagined him lifting the rocks out of the isthmus to let the Atlantic in, and piling them up on either side to form the Pillars of Hercules - *Mons Calpe* (Gibraltar) on the northern side, and *Mons Abyla* on the southern side, overlooking the Spanish colony of Ceuta (one of Spain's two equivalents of Gibraltar of the Moroccan coast, the other being Melilla).

We must get back to Solie and the part she played as junior hostess at Convent dinner parties. The great dining-room, which I described earlier, seated twenty-six, and on most occasions twenty-six plus Solie sat down to dinner. Solie took the preparations very seriously - too seriously for the staff's liking! Her self-imposed responsibility was to check that the table was set and the flowers arranged to her liking. The trouble was that she never gave warnings of her intention to inspect. Sergeant Feeney, who had supervised the table laying and had done the flower arranging for some twelve years, was aghast to find one evening after he had done his final check that some of the two dozen or so candles were no longer standing vertically in their candelabra as he was sure he had left them. And horror of horrors, one was lying cracked on the table. I don't think he was gullible enough to blame the wind. From then on, he locked the doors of the dining-room after laying was complete. He was well aware that Solie was an expert at opening any door that was not properly shut: indeed, such doors were the type of challenge that she could not resist.

Guests always arrived between 8 and 8.15 p.m., and Joan and I would receive them as they entered the large drawing-room. Outside in the corridor there was a small table upon which the seating plan was displayed in an ornate frame.

Chief Petty Officer Partington, who ran the administration of the Convent, showed the guests where they would be sitting at the dinner table, and politely asked the senior guest to remember that it was his duty to leave first at around 11.30; and, if there was a priest or nun amongst the guests, warn them that I would be asking him or her to say grace.

The positioning of the small table with the seating plan on it was very important to Solie. There was a sofa on the opposite side of the corridor, under which she could sit and view the guests without being seen. Like the flower beds around the fountain in the patio, she could use the sofa as her vantage point from which to select her partners for the evening.

Solie learnt very quickly that it was most unwise to join us in the drawing-room before dinner because we all remained standing while sipping our pre-dinner drinks and talking about the events of the day. There was too great a danger of being trodden on by mistake. Instead, she would join us when the great, heavy double doors of the dining-room were opened and Chief Partington came to tell me dinner was served. It was always a splendid sight. Looking through the two sets of double doors, you saw the great hall with its long table set with its silver and glass, surrounded by its blue leather backed chairs emblazoned with the Royal Arms, and only lit by its flickering candles. And at the far end of the room, framed by the pennants of all the past Governors, was the specially lit portrait of the Queen in her coronation robes.

As Her Majesty's representative, the Governor should always lead the way into the dining-room, but it was often a moot question as to whether I would, in fact, be doing so, or whether the first through the open doors would be Solie. She would rush in with her tail erect, looking very much the hostess leading the way, despite all the rules of protocol!

At one of our first dinner parties, Lady Spry, wife of the Chief Justice was sitting on my right and Lady Hassan, wife of Gibraltar's long serving Chief Minister, was on my left. After grace had been said by the late and much loved Bishop Rapallo, and we had all sat down, Lady Hassan bent forward and said to me in a confidential whisper:

'Isn't it a pity that we no longer have the Ceremony of the Keys at Convent dinners?'

My ears pricked up and I asked what the Ceremony had consisted of and why it had been stopped.

'Its a long time ago now.' Lady Hassan replied, 'When we had only generals as governors, the Keys used to be brought in by the Port Sergeant at the beginning of every dinner party. I think the admirals and air marshals felt that it was an Army custom, which was inappropriate for them to follow.'

I made enquiries later, but could find no-one who knew why the ceremony had been dropped nor how it was performed. I assumed that my two immediate predecessors, who were the first sailor and airman to hold the post, felt that it was incongruous for them to inherit General Elliott's mantle. Now that the first cycle of Army, Navy and Air Force governors had been completed and there was another general, myself, back in the Convent, I decided that the custom should be revived.

But what did the ceremony consist of and how was it carried out? Lady Hassan could describe it in a general way, but her memory of the details some six years after it was last performed was not clear enough for me to be sure that we could get it right. Sooner or later some old hand from the past would come to dinner and comment on how the ceremony had changed, probably for the worse!

Sergeant Feeney, that fount of knowledge about the Convent, came to my rescue. He had been a junior footman in the days of the last soldier governor and he was pretty sure that he knew most of the details. He could do even better than trust to his own memory. He knew one of the retired Gibraltar Regiment Port Sergeants, whom he was sure would be delighted to advise me. Then after further thought he said:

'Sir! You know the widow of General Sir Kenneth Anderson's, who was Governor just after the War, is living quite close to the Convent. She would tell you all about it.'

Why had I not thought of her? I kicked myself and then asked the ADC to invite Lady Anderson, who was in her eighties, the retired Port Sergeant and the actual Port Sergeant,

116

Sergeant-Major Saunders, to meet me for a drink one evening in the Convent dining-room to work out the revived ceremony.

I think our combined efforts at memory recall recreated the 'Keys' at Convent dinner parties as near to the original as possible. Lady Anderson added a special gloss:

'But, of course, Kenneth belonged to a Scottish regiment,' she said, 'He had a piper instead of a drummer to play in the Keys.'

I was tempted to say that as a former Queen's Gurkha Engineer Colonel that I could ask my regiment to provide me with a piper. Indeed, I had thought, at one time, of asking for a complete Gurkha house staff, but, although the regiment would have been delighted to provide me with one, I decided not to do so because I felt they and their families would find life strange and lonely in Gibraltar.

At our next dinner party the Ceremony was re-established. No one has since said 'I'm sorry, your Excellency, you've got it all wrong', so I can only conclude that it must be as near right as makes no matter.

After grace has been said, the company sits down. As they are opening their napkins and thinking out how to start conversations with their table companions, the sound of distant drums can be heard coming along the Convent corridors. The great doors slowly open and a drummer of the Gibraltar Regiment comes in followed by the Port Sergeant carrying the Keys. Both are in the full dress of the regiment - white helmets, scarlet tunics, and navy blue trousers with the broad red 'artillery' stripe down the side.

The Port Sergeant is drummed in slow time round the long table. As he reaches its head under the Queen's portrait, the Governor stands up and turns towards him as he halts.

'Sir!' the Port Sergeant bellows, 'The Fortress is secure and all's well, Sir!'

With a loud jangle of gun metal, he thrusts the Keys forward at arm's length. The Governor seizes the great ring, on which they hang, and, after a studied pause, takes them with an equally loud rattle and lays them on their cushion in front of him, replying:

'Thank you, Port Sergeant. Good night, Port Sergeant.'

The drummer strikes up again, this time in quick time, and they march out of the room. As the great doors close behind them, any ice there may have been due to the formality of the occasion is broken. Even the shyest guest has something to talk about!

There was nothing else special about Convent dinner parties except for Solie's part in them, which was, of course, as unique as she was. She had decided in her own mind that she had two responsibilities: first, to make the more nervous guests feel at home as she did at lunch parties; and secondly, to help remind the senior guest when it was time to leave.

As at all traditional English dinner parties, the ladies leave the men in the dining-room to enjoy their port after the toast to Her Majesty has been drunk. After 'powdering their noses', they retire to the small drawing room for coffee and liqueurs. Solie was always waiting for them there, curled up on the most comfortable chair. (After I had re-introduced the Keys ceremony, she never stayed in the dining-room: the drums hurt her ears.) She noted who did not have the courage to make herself comfortable, sitting instead on the front edge of her chair. Two dark brown velvet paws quietly placed on her knees and, with a delicate leap, Solie would settle on her lap and purr as if to say:

'Don't worry; I'll look after you. Just stroke me!'

This had the miraculous effect of making the guest the centre of attention and conversation much easier than she ever expected.

We men always sat far too long over our port, and so Chief Partington instituted a series of signals to remind me how time was flying. He would remove the port decanter stoppers as the ladies left the dining-room, and when he judged that they had waited long enough for us, he would put them back in front of me with an ostentatious flourish that no one could mistake.

As we all trooped back into the large drawing room, the ladies would rejoin us and the ADC's nightmare began, known as 'musical chairs'. He had to seat us in a way that ensured that we did not sit next to our dinner table neighbours, nor were husbands next to wives. This was relatively simple. His problems started about half an hour later when he had to use all his tact to persuade guests to change places again and ingenuity to ensure that everyone had someone new to talk to. Only the most careful preplanning would lead to complete success. Perhaps the most tactful way of putting it is that some ADCs had ways of conducting 'musical chairs' with more charm than others! I, as Governor, had the easiest job of all. When the time to change partners came, I sat still in the middle of the central three-seater sofa rather like a Sultan, and two new ladies were brought across to me to replace the first two!

At each change Solie had to change knees too. Her social instincts never deserted her. At the 'second change', she usually managed to select the wife of the senior guest and curled up on her knee, at the same time setting her personal time clock for 'twenty minutes'. When it rang in her head, she would jump down, arch her back and then stretch out full length before sitting upright on the hearth rug, facing the guests and signifying in a most expressive way that it was past her bedtime and time they all left. It often worked - bless her!

CHAPTER 10

SOLIE SITTERS AND OTHER FRIENDS

Solie had been in Gibraltar a year when she celebrated her second birthday. She was very much at home and was mistress of the Convent sub-world. The denizens of the skirting-boards, cupboards, nooks and crannies, and the gardens were under tolerably good order and feline discipline. They knew their places in Solie's order of things. She stood no nonsense from Fred, the tortoise, any longer. With a flick of her strong little paws she could turn him on his back as she did the terrapins, so Fred gave up chasing her and retired to the densest clump of foliage when she was about.

Fred only emerged when he knew he had our protection and a chance of acquiring a succulent lettuce leaf if we were having salad for lunch. He also had a passion for what he thought was 'glue' sniffing. The 'glue' he craved was the polish on my shoes. When I was reading in the garden, he would spend a happy half hour or so moving slowly round my shoes inhaling all the time! If, perchance, I was wearing crepe-soled shoes, he would go into ecstasy, taking small sucks at the rubber between sniffs of the shoe-polish! Solie did not approve. I think she was jealous!

Most of the Convent staff, other than the key personalities, Chief Partington, Sergeant Feeney and Sergeant Andrews, had moved on in the normal course of military postings. Solie could in all honesty claim to be the fourth longest serving and most experienced member of our household. Age and experience brought with it a desire for an established rigidity of routine. She liked to adhere to a fixed daily programme and expected others to do so too. The trouble was that Joan and I wanted to get away sometimes, and so had to leave her on her own in the Convent, which was never very popular as far as she was concerned.

At the weekends we had two alternative ways of 'getting away from it all'. We could either go up to the Governor's cottage almost a thousand feet up on the southern end of the Rock - or we could put to sea in the Governor's barge. The frontier was still tightly closed so there was no escape to Soto Grande or any other attractive spot in Spain as there is today. The cottage was our favourite because we could be entirely on our own with no footmen around and none of the clamour of the city to disturb us either. On the barge, however, there was always the crew in close attendance, and other small boats of every type around. After a year of life in the 'goldfish bowl' of the Convent, we both craved privacy at the weekends.

I never discovered when the cottage was built. It can be seen as a building of some sort on a detailed model of the Rock in the Gibraltar Museum, which is dated 1860. It stands on a secluded track cut into the face of the Upper Rock, and is cut off from the outer world with a high chain-link fence to ensure privacy. During the Second World War it was probably used as the officers' mess for O'Hara's 9.2 inch gun battery, which stands only a few hundred feet above it on the summit of the most southerly peak of the Rock.

The Governor's cottage of our day was not the original one used in the 19th Century and is often confused with it. The original was much lower down, just to the east of Europa Point. It is now known as Governor's Cottage Camp and has been occupied for some years by the Royal Engineers. In the old days, Governors and their complete households used to move out to that windy spot to reduce the chances of contracting Malignant Fever when epidemics were raging in the city. In 1804, for instance, some 6,000 people died out of a total civilian and military population of 15,000. These terrible epidemics of what was either yellow fever, typhoid or typhus went on until sanitation was improved in the 1870s.

We had to thank our predecessor's wife, Lady Grandy, for the present Governor's cottage. She had the building refurbished and turned into an ideal weekend retreat. We were most grateful to her. It had one long living room complete with log fire inside and verandah outside, double and single bedroom, shower-room and simple kitchen, so we could stay up there over night if we wished. On a clear day we could see the Atlas mountains across the Straits to the south, the Mediterranean stretching away to the horizon to the east, and the whole of the Straits as far as Tangier to the west. We could not quite see the Atlantic beyond Tangier because one of the headlands on the Spanish coast jutted out just too far.

The cottage had several other merits from our point of view, and one major disadvantage as far as Solie was concerned. Being high up on the end of the Rock, it was clear of the Levanter plume, and so was usually sunny whichever way the wind was blowing. And because the wind blows only east or west through the Straits and the cottage faced south, one or other end was always pleasantly sheltered. The disadvantage was that we dared not take Solie up there with us. We were often tempted to let her enjoy exploring all the rock crags and crevices, but there was no way of limiting her roaming area and the chances of losing her were too high.

Solie could not enjoy the barge either. Besides reminding her of her journey out in *Apollo*, which she had disliked intensely, there would have been too many risks in embarking her. We did not think she would enjoy a weekend at sea anyway. The barge was painted the traditional C-in-C's green. Apart from its official functions, it was well fitted with the usual facilities for all-day picnics and bathing parties. Its two powerful diesel engines gave it adequate speed, but she was a pig to handle. Commander Tom le Marchand, my Military Assistant, struggled valiantly to teach me how to manoeuvre her in a seaman-like way, but with remarkably little success. It was not his fault. I am just not designed for nautical pursuits. I do not know instinctively which is my left and right hand, let alone port and starboard; and I am quite capable of transposing east and west on a map, though not north and south, I am glad to say!

In our early days on the Rock we tended to use the barge when we had visitors. A picnic meal and plenty of liquid refreshment would be embarked, and we would set off after attending morning service in King's Chapel. The Rock, seen from the sea, is ever changing. From the Bay of Gibraltar, its benign western face looks like one of the somnolent lions at the base of Nelson's Column in Trafalgar Square. From the south it is a high razor backed ridge, often with its Levanter plume streaming out westwards off its peaks. And from the east, it is a forbidding palisade of rock, rearing up out of the sea in awful majesty, dwarfing all about it. This is the sight that so impressed mariners of classical times, who believed that *Mons Calpe,* as they called Gibraltar, marked the end of the known world: only demons lived beyond!

One of the reasons that we began to favour the cottage more than the barge as we gained more experience of the Rock's environment, was the uncertainty of being able to get round Europa Point in any comfort if there was much of a wind blowing. Calm seas around that point are the exception rather than the rule. The powerful tides rushing through the choke point of the Strait, whipped up by an opposing wind, can turn the sea into a maelstrom, which we and guests found very unattractive. Instead of being able to reach the clear calm waters off Governor's Beach on the eastern side of the Rock, we would be confined to the less salubrious waters of the anchorage and harbour on the western side.

I used to think, as many people did, that Governor's Beach was so named because it was reserved for the Governor and a select list of highly placed military and civic dignitaries. I noticed that the list did not include many Gibraltarian names, so I concluded that this was one of those anachronisms of our colonial past that should be rectified.

After dinner one evening, I asked the wives of two of the Government ministers, who were sitting either side of me on the sofa, what they knew of Governor's Beach. Did they think, I asked, that ministers and their families would like the privilege of being included on the exclusive list? I noticed only polite interest but no great enthusiasm for my suggestion so I did not pursue it. Indeed, I had forgotten all about it when we next landed on the beach from the barge. It is always said that kings, princes and governors never hear the truth; they have to search for it. Governor's Beach was certainly secluded and attractive, but how could you get to it except by sea? I roamed around and came upon the answer: a steep zigzag flight of steps ascended the almost vertical cliff face behind the beach. Full of enthusiasm I set off up them - one hundred, I counted, then two hundred, and yet I was still nowhere near the top. I discovered that it takes three hundred and forty-four of those steep steps to reach the locked iron gate on the track above the beach. No wonder ministers' wives and their families were not all that keen to be given the key to Governor's Beach!

Soon afterwards I found that the name Governor's Beach had nothing to do with the privilege of bathing there. During the Second World War, when there was a danger that Franco might help Hitler to attack the Rock, a secret route was constructed, by which couriers, landed from submarines, could come and go unseen, and by which the Governor and his staff could escape if the Germans succeeded where others had always failed in taking the Rock. The route ran from one of the caves behind the beach up through the labyrinth of tunnels inside the Rock to the underground Fortress headquarters. The steel door that covered the entrance in the roof of the cave, and the winch and bollards for securing the submarines can still be seen.

I have always been keen on fishing, so it was not long before the barge was taking me and my personal staff out fishing when the weather, tides and pressure of work allowed. The waters around the Rock have been almost fished out by Spanish trawlers, and the only sport to be had was in the waters off Europa point, which were too deep and rock strewn for their trawls. Solie was a lover of fresh fish so she approved of our trips, provided she was allowed her cut of our catch. Two new personalities entered our combined lives: Charles Bonfiglio and Sergeant Stone, who became my fishing gillies.

Charles in real life was a Treasury official, who knew Gibraltar's waters as well as any Scottish gillie. Solie loved him because whenever he was out with us the catch was good. No sport is ever worthwhile unless real skill is needed for success. Charles had the skills needed to fish off Europa Point where the tides and contrary winds oppose each other and are constantly changing. Moreover, it was not easy to fish at a depth of some sixty fathoms (360 feet) amongst the underwater crags that abound on the edge of the steep drop down into the 3,000 foot trench of the Straits. We had to use steel wire lines, about a pound of lead on each to carry the lines down through the currents, and electric reels to bring them up again from that depth. Even so it was a back-breaking business, hauling up a catch. The secret, which Charles tried to pass on to us, lay in how to find the rock ridges on the sea bed and to fish them without becoming snagged on them. The fish abound there because they can feed off aquatic debris carried by the tides and trapped by the reefs, but they catch fishermen's hooks just as easily!

Sergeant Stone entered our lives in a different way. The original sergeant driver of the Governor's Daimler, when we arrived, had a mild heart attack after taking us on a strenuous official tour of Morocco and had to be retired from the Gibraltar Regiment. Sergeant Stone was his replacement. He had been a Sapper in one of the Royal Engineer tunnelling squadrons, which, of course, commended him to me as a fellow Sapper. He had married a Gibraltarian girl, who, as is their wont, persuaded him to return to Gibraltar when he left the Sappers. He then joined the Gibraltar Regiment as a Gunner. He was not only an excellent driver and general handyman, but a keen fisherman and boat enthusiast as well. It was not long before he was not only in charge of the Daimler but of the barge as well!

Provided the wind and tides were right at weekends, we would slip out of the harbour in the grey light of dawn and come back in time for me to join Joan up at the cottage for lunch. She, like Solie, loved eating fresh fish, but would not have appreciated tossing about in the Straits all morning in the barge. If we had had a good day, we might come back with twenty or so assorted bream, blue mouth and various other types of Rock fish, most of which Joan and Solie enjoyed. As far as Solie was concerned the fresh fish meal in the evening made up for her lonely weekends spent in the Convent on her own.

We did not think that Solie really suffered much weekend loneliness, but Joan did feel that it was unwise to leave her on her own when we went back to England on leave. Such trips were far too infrequent for Joan's liking, and far too often for Solie's. We used to invite 'Solie-Sitters' to look after her when we were away for more than a couple of days. We had three willing volunteers, who were Solie lovers and delighted to be invited to stay in the Convent to look after her, or, as she saw it, to keep her company: Sheilah Way, the Matron of the Royal Naval Hospital; Patricia Smith, an active person in community affairs; and Mary Trippe, an elderly widow, who had spent much of her life in the social whirl of Tangier when it was an international city, and who was the life and soul of any party.

Each of our 'Solie-Sitters' enjoyed and suffered different facets of Solie's eccentricities. The first of Sheilah's many periods of guardianship was very worrying for her. Her charge arrived early one morning with a pronounced limp. Sheilah wanted to examine her left paw, was told rather rudely to mind her own business. She, Solie, was perfectly alright: just a slight sprain and nothing to get fussed about!

'Anyway you're only a nurse and not a proper doctor.' Solie seemed to say as she stalked out of the room with her tail defiantly erect, trying not to limp on what was clearly a very painful paw.

That was too much for Sheilah, who grabbed her and examined her paw whether Solie liked it or not. To her horror she found a large lump above the equivalent of Solie's wrist. Some years earlier Sheilah had lost a young cat of about Solie's age from cancer that had started in just the same place!

The snag about keeping pets in Gibraltar in those days was that there was no resident vet on the Rock. The RSPCA inspector ran an animal clinic, but he was not a qualified vet. Sheilah made enquiries and to her delight heard that there was a retired vet living in Gibraltar, called Spellman. She rang him up, fearing that she would be told that, as he was retired, he had no wish to be drawn back into the world of tiresome pets and hypochondriac owners even though it was the Governor's Cat that was in trouble.

Not a bit of it! Mr Spellman (I regret that I cannot recall his Christian name) was delighted to help. He loved Siamese and would come round to the Convent straight away, if Sheilah would warn the policeman at the front entrance to let him in.

Solie, snob that she was, accepted him straight away as a professionally qualified man of great experience. She liked his bed-side manner and offered him her paw for examination without any of the fizzing or rude cat words that she had used when Sheilah had tried to touch it. He thought that cancer was unlikely, and that there was probably a small chip of bone floating loose in her wrist, around which a cyst had formed. He could not be sure. It was a pity that the RSPCA did not have X-ray facilities with which he could check his diagnosis.

Sheilah was not a Royal Navy Matron for nothing. Indeed, when she was in her full Naval Matron's rig, she was as formidable a sight as one of Nelson's ships of the line with all sails billowing! She knew what to do. The Fleet Radiologist was out in Gibraltar at the time, carrying out specialist examinations on military personnel in the Royal Naval Hospital - Sheilah's hospital. Solie, as Governor's Cat, was certainly a very special military patient. After all, the Admiralty Board had accorded her a passage to Gibraltar in one of H.M. ships, and she was now resident in the Convent. The Fleet Radiologist agreed with a smile and fixed her an appointment with all the deference due to a member of the Governor's entourage.

And so it was that Solie became probably the first Siamese cat to be examined and X-rayed by so eminent a personage as the Fleet Radiologist in one of Her Majesty's Naval Hospitals. Mr Spellman's diagnosis proved correct. There was a small chip of bone in her wrist, probably caused by jumping down from some wall or other that she should not have climbed in the first place. There was now no other damage visible on the X-ray. Increased calcium intake was prescribed, which meant plenty of milk and at least one egg per day!

One egg per day was easier prescribed than administered.

Solie would not eat her egg. Sheilah found, however, that she was partial to the yoke but not the white. If she could get her started on the yoke, then she would continue lapping up the white as well. For the rest of our stay in Gibraltar, part of the Convent routine became the provision of a softly boiled egg for Solie at breakfast time, and part of her routine was to appear at breakfast time to demand her egg! I am glad to record that the swelling did eventually disappear, but Solie still demands her boiled egg to this day when I have breakfast here at West Stowell.

The egg routine in the Convent went smoothly until Patricia Smith took over as Solie-Sitter some months later. She was briefed on Solie's quirks, but she had a slight loss of memory on her first morning on duty. She had ordered a continental breakfast, and when the tray duly arrived next morning with the usual fruit juice, coffee and toast, there was Solie's boiled egg on it as well. Reading her copy of the *Gibraltar Chronicle*, the Rock's daily newspaper, she absentmindedly ate the egg, thinking no more about it until she heard a plaintive feline voice demanding 'Where's my egg?' The bell was rung and another egg was brought for a rather cross and impatient Solie.

It was some months before Joan found one day that the swelling had vanished. Mr Spellman came to examine her and declared that all was well. She was to continue her egg diet, but we could drop the milk as water is better for Siamese. We never did find out how she chipped one of her wrist bones in the first place. A night-duty policeman, patrolling in the grounds, did report that he had been scared out of his wits one night by a sudden flash of whitish fur as something rushed past him in the dark. He was sure it was Solie returning from a night out with the stray cats on Wellington Front, the bastion that lies between the Convent and the sea. Could she really be consorting, we wondered, with such undesirables, and had hurt her paw jumping down from the high Convent perimeter wall on her return?

Joan and I examined the wall very closely for places where she might be able to scale it. It was some twelve feet high, but its large, rough stones had been laid many centuries ago and so there were places with enough toe holds that might have enabled her to scramble up it. But surely she would not climb out to play with such gutter-snipes? We hoped not, but a little later we had reason to doubt our supposition.

Mary Trippe, Solie's third companion, taught her more about socialising than her mother, Easter Bunny, or those snobbish American Whites, who I am sure were Daughters of the American Revolution. Mary had lived in the gregarious environment of international Tangier for more than quarter of a century, and believed that everyone, including Solie, should enjoy life to the full. Mary's particular enjoyment was giving birthday parties. Whenever she was Solie-minding she would let Solie into a secret: it was her birthday. Whatever month of the year it happened to be, Mary had a birthday and invited all her closest friends to celebrate it in the very suitable surroundings of the Convent!

It was not until our last year in Gibraltar that Mary suddenly announced that she was going home to England especially to celebrate her 80th birthday. Solie confided to Joan that she thought that this time Mary's birthday was genuine. We agreed that Solie's female and feline intuition was serving her well!

Solie's clairvoyance was not matched by her maternal instincts. It came as no surprise that she did not welcome the arrival in the Convent of our first grandchild. Rosie, our daughter, brought out her three month old son, John Reid, whom the staff soon christened 'J.R.' with good reason! Solie would have nothing to do with him and absented herself whenever Rosie brought John in to see us.

One day quite a trivial incident occurred that led to a period of great anxiety in the Convent. Rosie had left John in his pram in the garden with a safety net over it. It was a good thing that the net was there because Solie's curiosity once again overpowered her disdain for John. She jumped up onto the pram, John screamed, and Solie ran for cover. It was a windy day and no one noticed that Solie had made for the nearest door, which happened to lead into the back yard of the Convent where the garages were situated. It slammed behind her, but nobody noticed that either.

That evening Solie was missing when we went to bed. I suggested that it was too soon to start worrying about her. She was sure to come in for her supper as soon as she was hungry. I was wrong. Next morning there was still no sign of her, so I ordered 'Cat-Smash', the equivalent of 'Sub-Smash' when one of H.M. submarines goes missing. The Convent staff swung into action. The policemen searched the gardens; the footmen looked into every room, cupboard and drawer; the cooks went through the kitchen, sculleries and pantries; the ADC notified the Police Station; and the whole operation was commanded and controlled by my new Military Assistant, Commander Jeremy Howard, who had by then replaced Tom Le Marchand. Not a trace of Solie could be found. Was she after all leading a double life: the high-born aristocrat by day and the Wellington Front gamin by night?

Joan and I spent a miserable day and a sleepless night after the abortive search. A second breakfast came and went with no Solie to eat the boiled egg waiting for her. It was Sunday morning and we were due to attend the St Andrew's Day service at the Church of Scotland in Governor's Parade. Joan decided rightly that she could not leave the Convent until she had news of Solie. By then she had been logged by the police as a missing person; the Gibraltar Broadcasting Corporation and the British Forces Broadcasting Service had both put out flash bulletins on the Governor's Cat, who was absent without leave; and the *Gibraltar Chronicle* had a short report on Solie's disappearance on its front page. There was just a chance that someone might ring up while we were in church with news of the miscreant, so Joan stayed by the phone while I went off to listen to our Scottish pastor, Stuart Phillips and to pray for Solie's safe return.

During Stuart's sermon, I heard a slight rustle at the back of the kirk. I saw Stuart smile and glance down at me in the front row, but I did not catch what he was trying to convey to me as he went on with his homily. It was not until the service was over and I was processing out with him, as is the custom for Governors to do at the end of a church service, that I saw Joan sitting in the back pew just inside the door. That could only mean one thing:

Solie had been found.

Back in the Convent, I held a drumhead court of enquiry. Solie stayed silent, determined not to incriminate herself. Joan gave evidence first. Her instincts had told her that the one area that might not have been searched properly, because Solie had never previously been 'catched' there, was the back yard and its garages. She cross-questioned the duty policeman, who assured her that he had looked into every garage and lock-up, calling 'Solie! Solie!' without success. However, the mental picture, which had formed in Joan's mind of a large strange policeman, calling 'Solie! Solie!' and shining a torch into potential hiding places, gave her the vital clue. If Solie was hiding in one of the garages, she would certainly not come out or even reply to a police summons. And so Joan had decided to carry out her own search of the back yard.

At first she had been no more successful than the policeman. She was on the point of giving up, when she asked what was in the last of the lock-ups, which used to be the Governor's cow-shed in earlier times. That was the wood store, she was told. It was said not to have been open all summer. Without much hope of finding the missing member of our family in there, she asked for it to be opened.

'About time too!' shrieked that small penetrating voice from somewhere amongst the piled logs, and out came a very dishevelled person with cobwebs around her ears, sawdust on her tail and her coat lacking its usual high gloss. The prodigal daughter had been found, and the fatted calf in the guise of a tin of her favourite cat-meat was opened and set before her!

The only evidence Rosie could give was that she heard John crying, thought she saw Solie rushing away, and heard one of the doors slam in the breeze. With no evidence from Solie herself, and with the rest circumstantial, I could but return an open verdict. Solie was back, and that was all that mattered.

No more would have been heard of the woodshed saga had it not been for an incident involving Mary Trippe and no lesser personage than the new Chief Justice of Gibraltar, Sir Renn Davis, who had recently succeeded Sir John Spry on his retirement.

Renn was a very eligible, but determined bachelor in those days, who, nevertheless, enjoyed female company. He had that senior bachelor habit of always being late at most functions, having no-one to keep him on time. I turned a blind eye to the occasions when he committed the breach of protocol by arriving after the Governor at social functions. Solie was not so forgiving and made a point of leaving her white hairs on his dinner jacket trousers when he dined at the Convent.

Shortly after the woodshed incident, we were holding a buffet supper in the ballroom in aid of, I think, the League of Hospital Friends. As usual Renn was late, this time because he had gone to pick up Mary Trippe, who was an equally unreliable timekeeper, to escort her to the party. Next day, I heard a rumour that I could not believe: Renn and Mary, it was said, had slept the night in his car parked in the Convent back yard!!

The real story was far less gossip worthy, but equally amusing; and it did go some way toward explaining Solie's unfortunate sojourn in the same place. When the buffet supper was over Mary and Renn stayed chatting to us and Solie for about twenty minutes or so after the last guests had left. Then Renn led Mary down to the back yard where he had parked his car. The wind in Gibraltar, as elsewhere, is no respecter of persons, even Chief Justices! As they passed through the same door into the yard that Solie had escaped through, it slammed behind them and, being fitted with a Yale lock on the Convent side, effectively cut off their retreat. To their horror, they saw the high exit gates out of the yard onto the street locked and barred. The police had locked up, assuming that the last guests had left and that Renn and Mary must be staying the night with us.

They both went round the yard calling and knocking at windows, but with no success. No-one heard them and they were, indeed, faced with the prospect of a cold night in Renn's car. But the Chief Justice, like Sheilah Way as Matron, was not Chief Justice for nothing. His investigative powers led him to discover a light alloy ladder tucked out of sight in one of the unlocked garages. He scaled the high Convent wall and sat on top of it, hoping to attract the attention of anyone, who would believe his story and summon the policeman from the guard-room at the front of the Convent to rescue them. No-one paid the slightest attention to the tall figure of the Chief Justice perched on the Convent wall! No motorist stopped and no pedestrian looked up, so Renn pulled the ladder up behind him and climbed down it into the street. Still nobody stopped him as he made his own way round to the front entrance of the Convent and secured Mary's release.

Solie could only purr with satisfaction that the incident showed that she was not the only person who could be caught out by the winds playing tricks around the Convent. Or was it the handiwork of the Convent's ghost, the Grey Lady, whom we will be meeting in the next chapter?

CHAPTER 11

THE GREY LADY AND ROYAL VISITORS

I mentioned, when explaining why the Governor's Residence is called the Convent, that there had been a nun associated with the Franciscan friary, whom Solie was to meet 'ere long. She was the Grey Lady, or rather her ghost, who roams the corridor outside guest rooms 19, 20 and 21 on the seaward side of the Convent. Room 19 is *her* room, because she is said to have been walled up alive in it, on orders of the Spanish inquisition, for breaking her vows.

The legend can never be proved or disproved. The seaward side of the Convent, like the west end of King's Chapel, was blown down so often during the many sieges that evidence of her immurement has long since been obliterated, but her ghost has been seen on a number of occasions in recent years.

Lady Anderson, who advised me on the Keys ceremony at Convent dinners, saw her when her husband was Governor in the late 1940s. Her grandchildren were playing in the ghost Corridor, while granny was sewing in the large drawing-room nearby. One of the children called out:

'Who's that lady, Granny?'

Lady Anderson was just in time to see the back view of a grey habited nun walking away from her down the corridor. The nun turned into Room 19, the door of which had always been kept locked because it had been turned into a store-room some years earlier for reasons I will recount later. When Lady Anderson reached it, she found that the door was, indeed, locked. She had it opened, but there was no one inside and the only window, from which there was a very considerable drop into the back-yard below, was securely fastened as well.

A little later Lady Anderson related her story to an eminent Roman Catholic prelate, who was staying in the Convent, saying that she was puzzled by the fact that the nun's habit was grey rather than the brown of the Franciscan Order.

'Did you not know, Lady Anderson,' he said to her, 'that the Franciscans wore grey in the 17th Century?'

Lady Anderson saw the nun again a little later. She was praying in one of the back pews of King's Chapel. At Lady Anderson's request a service of exorcism was held, which seemed to have laid the Grey Lady to a more peaceful rest. But, just before we arrived, Tom Le Marchand's son, Philip, was playing in the ghost corridor while his mother, Valerie, was in the drawing-room, helping to get the Convent ready for our arrival.

'Who was that grey lady?' Philip ask his mother, just as Lady Anderson's grandchildren had done some thirty years earlier. Valerie searched the corridors and rooms off them, but could find no one dressed in grey. Neither she nor Philip had heard of the Convent ghost at that time. They had only been in Gibraltar a few weeks.

There are various accounts of the Grey Lady, and of why she haunts Room 19 and the corridor outside it. The fullest is given in a book of short stories about Gibraltar by a military officer, Major Richard Hort, who wrote it to relieve the boredom of garrison duty in the mid-1800s. He recorded the tale as it was told to him in those days.

The Grey Lady was the daughter of a well-to-do Spanish family, who lived near Gibraltar, when the city and fortress were Spanish. She decided, against her father's wishes, to marry a man of whom the family - and particularly her brother - did not approve. One stormy night, this brother gathered her up, threw her onto his horse, and galloped off with her into Gibraltar. There he handed her over to the Mother Superior of the Convent of Santa Clara in Main Street, where the Montarik Hotel stands today. This convent had been founded in 1575. Being part of the Franciscan Order, it was under the spiritual discipline of the Monastery of St

Francis (The Convent today), and so the nuns were probably buried in its chapel (now King's Chapel).

The Grey Lady's lover was not to be deterred. He took the vows of the Franciscan Order and had little difficulty in persuading its authorities to send him to Gibraltar, a place which had been so unpopular in the 15th Century that Spanish kings were prepared to pardon malefactors prepared to settle there and help garrison the fortress. One of their decrees ran:

'We order and direct that all those willing to proceed to Gibraltar and to inhabit and dwell therein, whether they be swindlers, thieves, murderers. or other evil doers, or women escaped from their husbands, shall be freed and secured from punishment ....'

Soon after his arrival in Gibraltar, the lovers started meeting in the confessional of King's Chapel, and there they planned their escape. On the night of their escape, they abandoned their habits for ordinary clothes and started to make their way to the harbour where a boat was waiting for them. The alarm was raised and in the ensuing chase he slipped, trying to jump into the boat and was drowned, and she was arrested. She paid the penalty for breaking her vows somewhere near Room 19. Today Room 19 backs onto the ball-room, which was built on the ruins of the west end of the original Franciscan church, blown down in the Great 14th Siege of 1789-93.

During our first two years in the Convent, Room 19 remained a store-room as it had been in Lady Anderson's time. Years before, it had been the ADCs' room, but they had complained of a 'presence' in the room and a 'pressure' on them in bed at night. The fact that the 'presence' and 'pressure' might be female did not enthral them! One of General Anderson's more irascible predecessors had reacted to their complaints by allocating them the large room over the police-room at the front entrance of the Convent. They had exchanged ghostly female company for the constant chatter of the policemen below, and the noise of drunken parties in the early hours of the morning from the *Angry Friar* pub opposite!

Gibraltar was very much in the international limelight during our time there.   On occasions we found it quite difficult to accommodate large delegations of important people, who felt that they should all stay in the Convent. Our son-in-law suggested that we should bring Room 19 back into service as a single bedroom. Much to Rosie's horror and Solie's amusement, he volunteered to make the Grey Lady's acquaintance by sleeping in Room 19. He asked Solie to accompany him to act as his ghost-alarm, but she had other things to investigate that night and declined his invitation.

Next morning, the intrepid ghost-hunter reported sleeping well and was very disappointed, though inwardly relieved, that nothing had happened. If Solie could have spoken she would probably have asked Rosie:

'What religion is your husband?'

'Church of Scotland, you silly! But why did you ask?'

Solie would have kept her counsel, saying nothing as she had a theory to prove.

Governors are paid to take decisions after full and careful consideration of all the evidence and advice presented to them: Generals are trained to take decisions decisively and without hesitation. I decided to act in my latter capacity and ordered Room 19 to be redecorated and fitted as a single bedroom straight away. The work was to be completed in time for the arrival of an important NATO delegation in a fortnight's time. The whole party, consisting of Norwegian, Dutch, Belgian, Italian and Turkish officers of two star rank, was being looked after by a British colonel from a Scottish regiment. We could just give each member of the party a room to himself if the colonel slept in Room 19.

The day the delegation arrived, I swore the staff to secrecy about the Grey Lady. Our international military guests stayed two nights, and at breakfast on their last morning I asked the colonel how he had slept?

'Fine', he replied, 'It's a small but very comfortable room.'

Solie might have chipped in, asking him about his religion, but

I did it for her.

'By the way, what religion are you?' I asked.

'Oh! Free Kirk: why do you ask?'

Then I told him the story of the Grey Lady and the theory that Solie and now I were intent on proving. His sojourn in Room 19 had added new evidence for our researches!

Not long afterwards the Lord Mayor of London, Sir Peter Gadsden that year, came out with his entourage for a civic visit to the Mayor of Gibraltar. He brought with him the Sheriff of the City of London, the Chief Commoner, the Mace Bearer, and the Sword Bearer, all of whom were accompanied by their wives except for the Sword Bearer.

Again the Convent was at full stretch. The Sword Bearer was the obvious candidate for Room 19, in which he spent three undisturbed nights. Solie and I repeated our standard inquisition at breakfast on the last morning of the visit. The Sword Bearer had slept well every night, and we noted that he was Church of England.

So far so good! The next visitor to occupy Room 19 was the secretary to Archbishop Bruno Heim, the Pope's Apostolic Delegate to the Court of St James, and later the first Papal Nuncio in England since the days of Henry VIII. We put the secretary in Room 19 to be next door to the Archbishop, who was in Room 20, because the Royal Suite was being redecorated at the time.

The Archbishop's visit, like that of the Lord Mayor of London, was a great success: not only are most Gibraltarians practising Roman Catholics, but Bruno Heim was certainly highly charismatic. Most regrettably, however, we did not reach the final breakfast of his stay before the Grey Lady struck!

The first I realised that all was not well, was at about half-past seven on the last morning of the visit, when there was a loud knock on my bathroom door while I was shaving. I found Sergeant Feeney, standing in my dressing-room, in a state of high excitement:

'Surr!' he blurted out in his Irish accent as I emerged from the bathroom, 'The Grey Lady's been at it. She's sprinkled Holy Water over His Holiness's secretary!!'

I must confess that I did sniff the air in a quite unworthy attempt to detect whether Sergeant Feeney had been drinking or not. It was unworthy of me since I knew that the good sergeant had taken the pledge some years ago, and that, with a few minor exceptions that were not entirely his fault, he had stayed true to his vow.

I went along to Room 20, expecting to hear that someone had been hoaxing the secretary, because we had been discussing the legend of the Grey Lady at dinner the night before. Not a bit of it: the Archbishop was taking the matter very seriously. During the early hours of the morning, the secretary had been woken up by water being splattered over him. He switched on the light and looked up at the ceiling, expecting to see drips coming from a burst pipe or an over-flowing gutter, which can happen in old buildings like the Convent. The ceiling was dry!

The Archbishop had shown equally unworthy suspicions by lifting off the upturned glass from the water carafe beside the secretary's bed and smelling it. There was no trace of anything untoward there. Moreover, the carafe was still full and had obviously been untouched. The side of the bed was wet and so was the bed-side carpet. Where the water came from has never been explained, but the theory that I and Solie had been developing had received decisive confirmation:

'She *would* do it to a Catholic, wouldn't she?' we both said, looking knowingly at each other. The Grey Lady had every reason to dislike Roman Catholics after her treatment at the hands of the Holy Inquisition!

One thing that the people of Gibraltar have always longed for is a visit by Her Majesty. I was naturally keen to see if a Royal visit could be arranged, although I feared that Spanish sensitivities and H.M.G.'s desire to improve Anglo-Spanish relations precluded such a thing until the 15th Siege of the Rock was lifted. Nevertheless, we did have two Royal visits during our time, though not by the Queen. The first involved the Grey Lady and might have disproved Solie's and my theories about her continuing dislike of Catholics and desire for revenge; but the second fortunately did not as it would have spoilt a very happy occasion.

The Grey Lady escapade occurred during the visit of Princess Alexandra, who came out with her husband, as the Patron of the Royal Naval Nursing Service. They occupied the Royal Suite, which thanks to their visit was being modernised, as I have mentioned, during Archbishop Bruno Heim's visit. I do not think it had been refurbished since Kaiser Wilhelm II slept in it during his visit in 1906! The bathroom still had the large enamelled cast-iron bath and cumbersome porcelain basins and loo that he must have used; and the whole suite was festooned with archaic Victorian curtain fittings, plumbing and wiring.

In normal circumstances, when members of the Royal Family are staying in the Convent, their personal protection officer sleeps in the 'Detective's Room' next to the Royal Suite. On this occasion, the rules were waived to allow Miss Dawson, the Princess's personal maid, to be readily available to her. The frontier was still closed so the risks to the Princess's security were minimal. I might have allocated Room 19, the only other single room in the Convent, to the detective, but fearing that he might be a Catholic, I directed that he should be given the greater luxury of Room 20.

Solie, who befriended Miss Dawson, must have told her all about the Grey Lady; or, of course, it may have been Sergeant Feeney, who would have left nothing to the imagination in telling the tale. Anyway it seems Miss Dawson saw an opportunity to pay off some old score with the detective! What happened during their second evening in the Convent may be apocryphal, but it adds nicely to the saga of the Grey Lady.

The Royal party, including the detective, came back late that night after a dinner in the Wardroom of H.M.S. *Rooke*, the naval shore establishment in Gibraltar. The main corridor of the Convent, leading to the Royal Suite was well lit, but the way to Room 20 was in pitch darkness. The detective could not find the light switches so used his cigarette-lighter to find his way. The first thing he saw in the flickering light was a pair of small bright eyes at the end of the ghost corridor, which vanished immediately. Undeterred, he reached his room, and as he had an early start next day, he was soon in bed.

I should explain that Rooms 19 and 20 are connected via the bathroom shared by both rooms. The detective had checked that the bathroom door into Room 19 was locked on the far side and so had not bothered to bolt it on his own side. I should also explain that the windows, shutters and doors in the Convent all rattle in the slightest breeze. As the detective switched off his bed-side light, he noted that it was a bit windy outside so he did not worry when he heard a door or window creak in the direction of the bathroom.

Then he heard an obvious rustle and saw the unmistakable figure of the Grey Lady silhouetted against the pale glow of the city lights shining through the curtains of the window! The bathroom door creaked again and he thought that he heard the bolt slide home. Being a man of great presence of mind and quick reaction, instead of giving chase through the bathroom, he slipped out quickly into the ghost corridor. Miss Dawson and Solie found it difficult to explain why they were in that corridor so late at night, especially as Miss Dawson was carrying a shawl under her arm in mid-summer!

Everyone, especially Solie, enjoyed the Princess's visit. She stole the heart of every Gibraltarian who saw her. She was one of our easiest guests in the Convent during our time in Gibraltar. She was so considerate and so appreciative of everything that was done for her. Solie loved her; and so did we all.

Gibraltar suffered a terrible blow the following year when we heard that the Queen would be visiting Italy and would then be sailing in the Royal Yacht *Britannia* to Tunis and then on to Morocco, passing close to Gibraltar when *Britannia* sailed through the Straits, bound for Casablanca. We all hoped, and I certainly suggested, that, after her visit to King Hassan, she should transfer from *Britannia* to an aircraft of the Queen's Flight at Gibraltar for her flight home, staying a few hours on the Rock, if not overnight.

Excitement and hopes were high in Gibraltar at the prospect of a visit by the Queen. No one believed that she could pass so close without setting foot on the Rock before flying home. The Foreign Office, however, was adamantly opposed to her doing so. It might upset the delicate balance in Anglo-Spanish relations; and might stop the opening of the frontier, which the Spanish Government had agreed to do under the terms of the Lisbon Agreement, which they were hesitating to implement. Many sensible Gibraltarians saw the force of these arguments, but we were all desperately disappointed that no visit could take place. We could only hope that another opportunity would arise when the frontier had been opened. As it turned out Spain failed to honour the agreement anyway, but the Foreign Office were not to know that at the time.

In fact, the Foreign Office's caution was soon shown to be justified. We were all thrilled to hear that the Prince and Princess of Wales were to set off on their Mediterranean honeymoon from Gibraltar. They would fly out to us and transfer to *Britannia* for their cruise. As soon as the announcement was made, the Spanish Royal Family cancelled their attendance at the wedding; and the local Spanish authorities in the area around Gibraltar started organising demonstrations against the Royal visit, which included planning the obstruction of *Britannia*'s passage out of the harbour by a blockade of fishing vessels in the Bay of Gibraltar.

The King and Queen of Spain certainly did not attend the wedding, but the Spanish people were so entranced seeing it on television, that they forgot all about demonstrating at the frontier and blocking *Britannia*'s exit from the harbour. Instead, they followed Gibraltar's example and did everything they could to give the Royal couple the happiest possible send off on their honeymoon cruise.

Solie was disappointed, as we all were, that there would not be time for the Prince with his new Princess to stop at the Convent on their way from the airport to *Britannia*, which was berthed at the Naval Base. Nevertheless, she took a keen interest in the unusual preparations that were going on around her, and perhaps inspired Joan to make one splendid suggestion, which was acted upon.

Britannia arrived a couple of days before the start of the cruise. Admiral Greening, who was commanding her, came to dinner in the Convent that evening. I happened to ask him what course he would be taking after leaving harbour because we had to make arrangements to stop small boat loads of happy Gibraltarians, intent on waving the couple *bon voyage*, from getting in her way. The Admiral suggested staying close in shore until he reached Europa point so that as many people as possible could see her as she sailed away. He would then turn due east into the Mediterranean, giving no clue as to his likely destination to the mass of hungry journalists ready to pounce on the flimsiest scrap of evidence that would enable them to anticipate the itinerary.

I saw that Solie was on Joan's lap and seemed to whisper something to her. Joan took whatever hint it was and said:

'Oh! the people of Catalan Bay will be disappointed. They have decorated their village most beautifully. Couldn't you sail right round the Rock before you turn eastwards?'

Catalan Bay is a small village on the east coast, almost under the water catchments, and is inhabited like most isolated places by great individualists, who take an immense pride in everything that they do.

Admirals are not men who change their plans very readily or do so without reference to their staff, but Paul Greening promised to see what could be done.

The most difficult problem that we faced was finding a suitable car at short notice in which the Royal couple could been seen as they drove from the airport to the ship. There was no time to ship one out from England. Having been under economic siege for so long, Gibraltar's car population was getting long in the tooth, and having no opportunity to drive on the trunk roads of Spain, there was no call for large open cars.

'Brammy' Benatar, a Gibraltarian businessman, came to our rescue. He had an open Triumph Stag that had barely been used, though he had had it for some years. It was in pristine condition, but a bit cramped and very low in the back. We had specially raised seats fitted, and provided the car with a suitably large flag staff on the front bumper for the Prince's standard. Small though it was, it had just the right sporting touch for a young couple off on their honeymoon, even though they were the Prince and Princess of Wales.

There was no doubt about who should drive the Stag. Sergeant Stone, my driver and fishing companion, cleaned and polished that car with loving care. Driving it on the day was one of the proudest moments of his career. Solie was just plain jealous of him!

When the great day came, Solie helped us to dress for the occasion. I was wearing a light civilian suit instead of uniform because we wanted to make the occasion as happy and informal as possible, and so Solie had no spurs to paw or blue trousers to decorate with her hairs. She gave me up and went to help Joan. Then Chief arrived and promised to hold her up on the Convent balcony to see the Prince and Princess drive by.

The next two hours were an unforgettable dream to the people of Gibraltar and us. And although it is all over, it remains a dream to be savoured as the years pass, and time turns it into legend.

The Prince was piloting the Andover of the Queen's Flight when it touched down in a perfect landing at R.A.F. North Front, Gibraltar's airport. Joan and I greeted the couple as they came down the steps of the aircraft and introduced them to the political leaders and senior officials. When we walked over to the cars, I stopped momentarily to point out the features of the Rock so that the Press could take pictures of them with the towering cliffs of North Front in the background. It worked and the Press were very grateful.

We drove slowly through Main Street in what was a security man's nightmare, but a people's dream. The city erupted in a surge of emotion. The couple were so obviously in love that it affected even the hardest of cynics. All the buildings were decorated with Union Jacks and draped with red, white and blue bunting. Many people in the crowds that packed the narrow pavements, weeping with happiness as well as cheering, had

144

dressed in the same colours for the occasion. From every window and roof top came a shower of confetti. Some people were so excited that they threw their confetti boxes as well!

'Good!' said the Prince above the roar of the crowd as a box hit Sergeant Stone. 'They are lowering their aim.' The Royal couple had already been hit several times!

We reached *Britannia* exactly on time, thanks to Sergeant Stone's accurate driving. The Prince graciously invited Joan and me, and the Chief Minister and Leader of the Opposition with their wives, on board for a farewell drink as *Britannia* made ready to sail. When we had disembarked, she edged slowly away from the berth and the Prince and Princess emerged on the after deck, holding hands and waving as vigorously as we were on shore. And on the quay, the band of the resident battalion and, on board, the Royal Marine band both struck up 'God Bless the Prince of Wales'.

Britannia gathered speed as she sailed majestically down the harbour with the Prince's standard, Admiral Greening's flag and the Trinity House flag at her three mastheads. Out of every berth and mooring in the harbour came an armada of boats of all shapes and sizes, which gathered around her to escort her to sea. Royal Marine high-speed craft and our police launches kept them at a safe distance from *Britannia*'s wash, but it was a miracle that no boat capsized and no one was hurt.

True to his promise, Admiral Greening sailed close inshore right round the Rock until he reached Catalan Bay. As *Britannia* turned eastwards and began to disappear in the gathering dusk of that great day, those on shore with field glasses could see two figures still standing close together on the after deck.

We all went to bed happy that night as I am sure that they did. Next morning Sergeant Stone showed us the Stag. Its floor must have been three or four inches deep in confetti.

Joan had it all packed into small plastic bags. Its sale made her favourite charities a little bit richer.

We had another cause for celebration a few days later. Chief Partington passed his promotion exams, and it was announced that he was to be promoted Fleet Chief in three months' time. We feared that this would mean his leaving the Convent. Their Lordships in the Admiralty, however, smiled and agreed that he should stay with us until the end of our time on the Rock. Joan and I were very relieved. Solie was beside herself with delight: she had great confidence in Chief, and hated change.

CHAPTER 12

GUARD-MOUNTING
AND OTHER CEREMONIES

Solie and Fleet Chief had a love/hate relationship. As long as he had been a mere Chief Petty Officer, she felt that as Governor's Cat she could pull rank on him. Now that he was addressed as Mr Partington, she was not so sure. He was in total charge of the discipline of the Convent staff, which she feared might include her; and he was also responsible for maintaining the high standards of everything to do with the Convent, particularly on ceremonial occasions. Solie must often have heard me mutter in moments of frustration 'If you can't beat 'em, join 'em!' She decided to follow the same policy in re-establishing her relationship with the new Fleet Chief. She would become his adviser on and critic of ceremonial affairs.

Every Monday at 10.30 sharp during our time on the Rock, there used to be the ceremonial changing of the Governor's Guard in Convent Square, which attracted large numbers of spectators, especially tourists. My successors changed it to Tuesdays for the benefit of the tourists, whose package holidays tended to start and end on Sunday. On the first Monday of their holiday, they might not have found out about Guard-Mounting or where it was held; and by their second Monday most of them would be on their way home. So Tuesday became Guard-Mounting day until the IRA took a hand in disrupting the peace of Gibraltar. Since the shooting of the three terrorists by the SAS, the ceremony has become less frequent because of the security risks involved.

The Governor's Guard was provided by the resident British

infantry battalion, but, on special occasions and when the battalion was training away from the Rock, the Gibraltar Regiment took over. What the arrangements will be when the resident battalion is withdrawn in 1991 was still undecided when Solie and I were writing this book.

Regimental reputations were made and just as easily lost at this weekly ceremony, at which perfection was the over-riding requirement. During our time there were three different resident battalions: 2nd Queen's from the Home Counties; 2nd Light Infantry largely composed of Geordies from Northumbria; and 1st Staffords (The Prince of Wales's) from the West Midlands.

Each battalion had its own very distinct and characteristic way of doing things, based upon its traditions that, in many cases, stretch back to Cromwell's New Model Army. Contrasts in style between battalions, and between companies within them, were never more evident than in Convent Square on Monday mornings.

Solie took a particular interest in two things. First there was the marshalling of the guests invited to accompany Joan and myself out onto the balcony above the Convent front entrance to watch the ceremony. And the second was the choice of music that the band would play during the parade. The two were closely inter-related since the tunes chosen had to be appropriate to the guests on the balcony. If Solie inspired the Bandmaster and Fleet Chief, then the guests were flattered, but mistakes could be made.

Monday's routine was simple. At 10.15, the guests would start assembling in the small drawing-room where Fleet Chief, with Solie in attendance, would brief them on what would happen and where each was to stand on the balcony. They rarely remembered their positions and had to be discreetly shuffled around by the ADC, which, to Solie, was all part of Monday's fun.

As long as the Queen's were with us, I could time my own movements with precision. I knew that once I heard their band coming up Main Street from South Port, I had time to stop whatever I was doing in my office, buckle on my Sam Browne, don my hat, pick up my gloves and leather covered cane, and arrive just at the right moment to lead the guests out onto the balcony. My position was in the centre under the flag staff from which the Governor's Union Flag flew from the mast-head, and the red and white City flag from the jack-stay.

Convent Square by that time would be packed with spectators, five or six deep. Solie would sit demurely as if counting the guests out, but rarely ventured onto the balcony herself because she knew from bitter experience that sometimes the drummers would put on a special display of drumming and that hurt her ears. As I took up my position, I used to look slowly round the sea of faces below to see that any of the senior citizens of advancing years, who attended the parade regularly, were still there so that I could acknowledge them with a smile or ask after their health later if they were absent.

Looking left up to the top floor flat of the apartment block over the Copper Kettle tea room, I would expect to see Miss Vera Bentubo with a party of her own guests watching from her windows. She was a great character, who served on almost every charity committee, but age did play tricks with her memory. On the pavement below the late Major Jack Ellicott, one of the first elected members of the old City Council, always stood watching the parade with a very experienced eye. One Monday he was missing: my enquiries revealed that sadly he had just died.

Further round the square there would be a small, wizened septuagenarian couple called Palmero. He used to bring a little wooden stool for his wife to sit on, and had a habit of conducting the band with his pipe and singing at the top of his voice when he knew the words of a particular march. He was a delightful old rogue, who knew that his display of loyalty would bring its rewards. One Monday I noticed that he was conducting with an empty hand: no pipe!

Next day he had a new one with Solie's compliments!

On the right-hand side of the square, near the Angry Friar Pub, stood the younger, bearded figure of Major Momy Levy, the nephew of the Chief Minister, Sir Joshua Hassan, and a great enthusiast and supporter of all the traditions of British Gibraltar.

Despite his beard, he had the distinction of commanding the 9.2 inch coast defence guns on the top of the Rock when they fired for the last time before being de-commissioned in the mid-1970s. Little did he know that I was the Quartermaster-General, who had been instrumental in their active retirement. They were bringing down the ceilings of the married quarters that my Department of the Ministry of Defence had just built near Europa Point, and they had been outdated by *Exocet* missiles any way.

And in the front of the crowd, all round the square, there were little groups of children from the infant and primary schools. One group used to arrive like a team of Alpine climbers, all roped together in case one got lost!

But the most important section of the crowd from the battalion's point of view was the Guard-Mounting Fan Club, which used to gather between the Copper Kettle and the Guard-room. Sometimes the tourists were a bit slow in applauding the efforts of the band. The Fan Club triggered applause by clapping vigorously just at the right moment. They were able to do so because, as Solie knew, they were all in the know. The Club's members were the wives of those most involved in the parade: the Fortress Commander; the CO of the battalion; the Staff Captain, who was responsible for the correctness of the ceremony; the battalion's Adjutant, who was on the parade; the Chaplain, who was probably praying that all would be well: and my Military Assistant, who would be noting anything amiss.

The Old Guard was always formed up in the square as the New Guard marched in behind the band. The Old Guard Commander would bellow out in a stentorian voice:

'Governor's Old Guard, provided by ...... Company; one sentry by day; all's well.'

The reply would ring back:

'Governor's New Guard, provided by ...... Company; one sentry by day'. The 'all's well' was omitted as the New Guard Commander could not tell what unexpected events might occur during his week on duty.

The band would then start its display and Solie and Fleet Chief would know whether their choice of music was a success or not.

When we had a senior naval officer on the balcony, *Hearts of Oak* or *Anchors Away* would be appreciated. I was never certain whether *Those Daring Young Men in their Flying-Machines* went down particularly well with Air Marshals. The late Lord Chief Justice Widgery was highly amused by the choice of *The Lord High Executioner*, but the Inspector of Overseas Constabulary from the Foreign and Commonwealth Office was less enthusiastic about *A Policeman's Lot is not a Happy One*.

Solie and Mr Partington pulled off the greatest coup on the day that Port Stanley fell at the end of the Falklands Campaign in 1982. The crowd cheered its lungs out as the band struck up with a medley combining *Don't Cry for Me Argentina*, *Rule Britannia*, Toreador from *Carmen*, and the pop tune, *The Little White Bull*. Their worst failure was to select *The Yellow Submarine* for a very senior submariner: he was not amused!

After the Old Guard had marched off behind the band, I would lead the guests into the balcony room, where Fleet Chief would be waiting with glasses of chilled white wine in summer or warmed claret in winter. The Brigadier, the CO and the duty company commander, who were always in attendance, could then uncross their fingers and toes if all had gone well.

Solie would be there too, looking her most attractive and helping everyone to relax.

We and, I think, the people of Gibraltar, found the changes of battalion rather disconcerting at times. We had hardly got to know Chris Champion's 2nd Queen's than they were relieved by Tim Bevan's 2nd Light Infantry. Tim's father had taught me to write English at Shrewsbury in the 1930s. His son was a large man in every way, both in physique and personality, and his battalion reflected his determination to do well as resident battalion while, at the same time, enjoying their time in the Mediterranean sun. They did both and woke the Rock up in the process!

2nd Light Infantry's first Guard-Mounting was a warning to me and Solie that the shape of things had changed. Perhaps we were slow to appreciate the effect that the arrival of Light Infantry would have on our routine. I was standing in my office by the French window that leads into the garden, having a few words with Solie about being kinder to Fred, the tortoise, whom I had found on his back with his small stumpy legs flailing the air, much to Solie's amusement. He could right himself on the flat stone paths, but this time she had upturned him in a softish flower-bed. The soil gripped his shell just too much for him to get back onto his feet.

Solie, Fred and I heard the sound of the Light Infantry band, starting off with the New Guard from South Port. I turned Fred gently back onto his feet, walked into my office, and donned my belt and hat, confident that I had plenty of time to reach the balcony. Then I realised that the band's music was different. Bugles and not drums predominated, and the sound was approaching at an alarming pace. The crescendo of the bugles told Solie that attending Guard-Mounting would not in future be included on her weekly schedule; and it warned me that I would not be on the balcony in time, if I did not break into a trot. I was just in time. As I took my place under the flag staff, the band and New Guard swung into the square, marching at twice the normal pace as is the custom of the regiments of the Light Division. Like Waterloo, my arrival on the balcony was a close run thing!

The other problems were caused by the Light Infantry's change of pace. 2nd Queen's Guard-Mounting had taken well over twenty minutes. Tim's first performance took less than fifteen! His battalion's drill movements were carried out with far fewer words of command and, like their marching, at twice the pace. This was fine for waking up the sleepy hollows of the Rock, and deterring Solie from attending Guard-Mounting, but it was not acceptable to the tourist industry.

The tourists would not be getting their money's worth!

A solution was not difficult to find. The band would play two pieces instead of one while stationary at the beginning of the ceremony, and it would double the number played when it was counter-marching in slow and quick time. This pleased everyone except Solie, who wanted the bugles eliminated all together. She did not attend Guard-Mounting again until Ian Freer's 1st Staffords arrived a year later. Then we did not change the band schedule, so the Staffords' Guard-Mounting lasted a full half hour; the tourists had more for their money; and the children were delighted to be away from school for a few minutes longer.

2nd Light Infantry's farewell to the Rock will be long remembered. As the finale to their Queen's Birthday parade, which took place just before they left, Tim, whom I have said was a very large officer, doubled his battalion off 'en masse' with companies abreast in close column with himself, followed by the regimental Colour party, at their head. They were all in their ceremonial summer dress with white jackets and green trousers, and made a splendid sight with the dust of the parade ground swirling up in the breeze behind them. A few days later, he led his battalion through Main Street where the Mayor took their farewell salute. By way of contrast, they were in full battle order, marching at Light Infantry pace and with all their heavier support weapons carried in their Land Rovers at the rear of the column. They looked and were a highly efficient fighting formation.

Nonetheless, it was with some relief that the people of Gibraltar and, of course, Solie welcomed Ian Freer's Staffords. The pace of the Light Infantry at work and play had almost been too much for the Mediterranean environment. Ian had been my Staff Captain when I was Quartermaster-General, so we knew him and his Australian wife, Karla, very well indeed. Solie had not been born then, but she liked the Staffords. The re-assuring roll and pace of their drums was less jarring to her ears than the high pitched urgency of the Light Infantry bugles. And the civilian inhabitants of the Rock, especially those who lived over the many pubs in the city, found the nights less noisy, except when the Fleet was in.

Ian's Staffords were no less efficient than Tim's Geordies, but they were different in temperament and traditions. The Staffords were from the undemonstrative agricultural shires of the West Midlands: 2nd Light Infantry hailed from the fast talking, bustling industrial cities of the Tees and Tyne in the North East. And the Staffords were a Regiment of the Line with all the attributes of the steady, imperturbability of Britain's 'Thin Red Line'; whereas the

Light Infantry's tradition is of the rapid skirmishing actions in front of the Line.

The Staffords came into their own carrying out the Ceremony of the Keys in Casemates Square, and, as I will describe later, during the Falklands War when the Rock was on full military alert in case some ambitious Spanish general tried to make himself a national hero by taking Gibraltar in a surprise attack to avenge the defeat of their Argentinian cousins.

The Ceremony of the Keys depicts the nightly posting of the outpost platoon outside the Land Port, the only gate that the Spaniards could possibly reach during the Great Siege of 1789-93. Each evening, the Port Sergeant would report to General Elliott for the Keys with which to open the Land Port so that outposts could be positioned to give warning of the approach of any Spanish force intent on using the cover of darkness to assault the northern fortifications.

The Ceremony was only performed twice in the Spring and twice in the Autumn of each year. Winter was out of the question since the weather was too unpredictable; and summer was too hot. I was once foolish enough to be persuaded by the Minister for Tourism to agree to a fifth 'Keys' in early June because the P & O cruise liner *Canberra* would be in port. Apart from P & O, no one else was very pleased with my decision to break with tradition. The Commissioner of Police complained about having to clear Casemates Square, which was the city's main car park, and the whole of Main Street on two more occasions - once for the rehearsal and again for the real thing. It took most of his force all day to ensure success. The Financial Secretary complained about the costs; and Fortress Headquarters grumbled about there being no precedent for a fifth 'Keys'. The only people, who did not question the Governor's decision, were the Staffords. Their traditions would not allow them to be deterred by such a minor consideration as heat on a ceremonial parade.

The Governor arrives at Casemates in the Daimler, carrying the Keys, and mounts the saluting dais for the Royal Salute. Then the ceremony follows the normal routine for any 'Beating Retreat' ceremony. When 'the evening gun' is fired at sunset, as it used to be every night in Gibraltar until after the Second World War, the Union Jack and City Flag are lowered, and the sound of the fifes and drums of the Gibraltar Regiment are to be heard entering the Square with the Port Sergeant and the escort for the Keys behind them. The Port Sergeant halts in front of the Governor and bellows:

'May I have your permission to secure the Fortress, Sir?'

The Governor replies by thrusting the Keys forward with a rattle, and the Port Sergeant takes them. He then marches off at the head of the outpost Platoon into the tunnel in the corner of the Square that leads through walls to the Land Port. After a short pause, symbolising the posting of the outposts for the night, the Keys and their escort are marched back up Main Street by the two bands.

There is just enough time for the Governor to drive back by another route and to be ready to receive the Keys back from the Port Sergeant at the entrance to the Convent. Like Guard-Mounting, it can be a close run thing! The ceremony ends with the Governor turning to Fleet Chief, who takes the Keys and carries them back to their cushion in the dining-room.

On the occasion of the 'fifth' Keys in early June, it did not seem a particularly hot evening, but as I arrived on the dais I realised that instead of the sun being about to dip below the horizon as it would have been in March and April, or in September and October, it had some way to go and it was shining straight in the eyes of the Escort Platoon, drawn up and ready for my inspection at the start of the parade. Their turn-out had been immaculate, but perspiration was now running down their faces; large damp patches were appearing on their white tunics; and they were having to pucker their eyes up in the glare of the sun. Yet not a man moved. The Staffords were as steady as their forbears had been at the terrible battle with the Sikhs at Ferozeshah in the 1800s, at Ypres in the First World War, and at Arnheim in the Second, to name but a few of the Battle Honours on their Colours.

When I returned to the dais, it was my turn to stand still and curse the day that I gave into commercial pressure to mount a fifth 'Keys' in summer. My earliest lessons in applied physics came back to haunt me as I stood on the dais watching the band carrying out its gyrations in the traditional way. The top half of me was encased in the starched white linen of my jacket, which reflected the sun quite efficiently, but the bottom half was in some of the best heat absorbing material available - tight fitting, navy blue serge. I have rarely been so uncomfortable, and I had only myself to blame. My annoyance was even greater when I realised that Solie's colouring was almost the same as mine in terms of heat reflecting qualities - white on top and dark brown below.

'Ah! but I am not foolish enough to stand out like that in the Summer sun', she might have said to me when I arrived back in the Convent. Instead she just rubbed a line of her whitish hair round my offending blue overall trousers, saying with a purr, 'Nice to see you back.'

The most moving ceremony of all on the Rock is the annual memorial service to those who died in the Battle of Trafalgar in 1805. It is held in the Trafalgar Cemetery, just outside South Port, where some of Nelson's men, who died from their wounds after being brought back to Gibraltar, lie buried. Most of those killed during the battle were, of course, committed to the deep. There are, however, many more headstones in the cemetery that record the deaths of men, women and children who succumbed to the epidemics of 'Malignant Fever'. Wreaths are laid on the actual Trafalgar graves, and today's sailors and WRNS are formed up amongst the tomb stones.

The Governor begins the service by reading Admiral Collingwood's despatch to General Fox, the Governor of the Rock in 1805:

'Sir;

Yesterday a Battle was fought by His Majesty's Fleet ... and a Victory gained, which will stand recorded as one of the most brilliant and decisive that ever distinguished the British Navy ... Our loss has been great in men, but what is irreparable and the cause of universal lamentation is the death of the noble

Commander-in-Chief, who died in the arms of Victory.'

The Flag Officer then reads Nelson's prayer, written just before the battle, and found in his cabin afterwards:

'May the great God, whom I worship, grant to my country, and for the benefit of Europe in general, a great and glorious victory, and may no misconduct in anyone tarnish it, and may humanity after victory be the predominant feature of the British Fleet .....'

The service ends with the Naval Hymn:

'Eternal Father strong to save,

Whose arm doth bind the restless wave,

Who bidd'st the mighty ocean deep,

Its own appointed limits keep;

Oh! hear us when we cry to Thee,

For those in peril on the sea.'

No one can be left unmoved, looking out from that quiet spot amongst the Mediterranean pines under the southern walls of the fortress that guarded Nelson's naval base, and to which H.M.S. *Victory* was towed after the battle in her dismasted state and carrying Nelson's body in its cask of rum.

The weather plays its part in the Trafalgar Day Service just as much as with the 'Keys', but in rather a different way. The date cannot be altered but the order of dress can be varied to suit the long range weather forecast for the year. It is the custom for the Admiral, who is expected to know all about weather, to decide when the three Services in Gibraltar should change from summer to winter uniforms. Trafalgar Day, the 21st of October, is right on the break point, and so it is not easy to decide the dress for the occasion.

Whatever classical deity controls the weather in the Straits, I am sure that it cannot be Neptune. He would be kind to eminent sailors like the Flag Officers, Gibraltar. It is rare for an Admiral ever to guess right. If he decides to change dress after Trafalgar Day, the whole company shivers in summer rig as a howling equinoctial gale rips through the cemetery; and, if he does the reverse, they invariably swelter in winter uniforms under a blazing autumn sun! Even Solie and Fred delay their decision on when to adopt their winter routine until after the Admiral has been proved wrong on Trafalgar Day!

There is another aspect to all these ceremonial events, which is equally hazardous. In all Crown Colonies, there is an Order of Precedence, signed by Her Majesty, which has to be adhered to on all formal occasions, ranging from the Queen's Birthday Parade at one end of the spectrum down to the Girl Guides' Thinking Day Service at the other. Anyone with official standing in the Colony has his or her place as clearly defined as the long experience of those who dealt with such matters in our imperial past could devise. Even so, it is not entirely foolproof as we soon found during our first year on the Rock. Indeed, problems were still cropping up as we left Gibraltar, because people and official posts are always changing and do not necessarily fit the rules devised for totally different conditions.

The trouble in Gibraltar is that there are really two different communities trying to act in unison. One knows the Precedence List backwards, and the other has barely heard of it, let alone understands it. The former are the Gibraltarians, who live nearly all their lives on the Rock, and know exactly who is senior to whom. The latter are the Service community, who are birds of passage, but now in our post-imperial era rarely live in colonial territories. They are used to their own hierarchical system and find it hard to understand that a Gibraltarian civilian, however well dressed and groomed, could possibly take precedence over, say, the Admiral in all his finery! In these democratic days, however, the elected representatives of the people do take precedence over officials at various levels. For instance, local Government Ministers come before the Service Commanders, a thing that would have been unthinkable twenty years ago, and has still to sink into many naval, military and air minds!

As I have already recorded, Solie was one of the worst offenders for breaking the rules of protocol. She had no place on the Precedence List, but her excuse for rushing into the dining-room ahead of everyone, including the Governor, was her inherent right of self-defence! She might be trampled under foot in the doorway, if she did not do so - or, at least, that was her excuse.

In our first year, we had a number of protocol flare-ups. Some dignitary would be seated in the wrong place at an official function, and would make his displeasure felt by ostentatiously walking out, muttering about unforgivable insults to himself and his wife. Next day, Tom Le Marchand would receive an irate letter, demanding an apology from whichever organisation had been responsible for the function. He always did his best to smooth ruffled feathers, and did haul offenders over the coals. Feeling that these letters suggested that he and his staff must be doing something wrong, he looked back through the files of earlier years and found just as many complaints and almost always from exactly the same people!

Our worst protocol nightmare occurred at the 1978 Battle of Britain Memorial Service in the Roman Catholic Cathedral of St Mary the Crowned. The R.A.F. officer in charge of seating arrangements was new to Gibraltar and had not been as well briefed by his predecessor as he should have been. Just about everything that could go wrong did do so. The Service Commanders were seated in front of the Government Ministers! This might have been excusable on the grounds that, after all, it was a Service occasion. Unfortunately, other senior guests' invitations showed only the row allocated to them, and no attempt had been made to allocate actual seats. In consequence, the first to arrive in each row took the aisle seats, and the more senior but later arrivals had to scramble past lower ranking officers to reach whichever inner seats remained unoccupied. Worse was to come!

There was a well established drill for bringing up V.I.P. cars at the end of any ceremonial occasion so that guests could be driven away in the correct order of precedence. As Joan and I left the Cathedral, I saw out of the corner of my eye the Admiral's flag on the car parked immediately behind our Daimler instead of the Chief Minister's. My heart sank. I suspected, though I could not see beyond the Admiral's car, that the Brigadier's and the Air Commander's cars would be next. Regrettably, my suspicions were over-optimistic. It transpired that all the Service official cars had been brought up in front of the Chief Minister's car. He had been in a hurry and had had to walk back to his office, followed by all his Ministers in justifiably high dudgeon.

Tom's subsequent inquiry revealed a simple, though inexcusable, explanation. The R.A.F. officer had handed to the Police Inspector in charge of car parking a list of cars in no specific order of precedence, but with the Service cars in a block at the beginning. In normal circumstances, the Inspector would have gone through the list with him and put the cars in the correct order, which he knew almost by heart. But circumstances were not normal. The Police Association, in which the Inspector happened to be an office holder, was in dispute with the Government over pay. The opportunity to show 'the withdrawal of good will' was too good to miss. He did nothing other than feed the cars forward in the order on the R.A.F. list!

After that I decreed that all protocol would be checked by Tom's experts: the Staff Captain in Fortress Headquarters responsible for ceremonial, my regular and three honorary ADCs and Mr. Partington. I threatened to hang the next offender from the Sovereignty Flag Pole on the highest point of the North Face at Rock Gun. Solie was told to keep her claws crossed to ensure no more protocol mishaps.

CHAPTER 13

JOAN'S AND SOLIE'S VIEW OF SPAIN

No light hearted account of our time in Gibraltar would be complete without a passing reference to Gibraltar's perennial political problem. Joan and Solie, like everyone else in Gibraltar, could never ignore the long-running saga of the Spanish pursuit of their claim to the Rock, and of their constant endeavour to persuade the world that Gibraltar should be returned to them in spite of the deep-seated objections of the Gibraltarians. It dominated almost every facet of our lives and waking moments.

Joan was always my most helpful adviser, but Solie, although a good listener, could only help me by telepathy. She would sit beside me on the desk upstairs in my study in our private suite, apparently watching the ships passing in the Bay below, but perhaps subconsciously inspiring me with some new ideas that I could use in the never-ending struggle to cajole Spain into adopting a good neighbour policy towards Gibraltar, and towards lifting the 15th and longest Siege of the Rock.

In the early days of our time in Gibraltar Joan's interest and Solie's curiosity led to them cross-questioning me on the problem. They wanted to know, as newcomers to the Rock, why a large piece of jagged limestone, sticking out off the southern coast of Spain should be British and not Spanish as geography would suggest? I had to give them and all our many visitors a short history lesson, which went something like this:

'For the first 750 years of the Rock's recorded history as an inhabited place, it was ruled by the Moors, as was the whole of southern Spain. The general, who led the Moorish invasion of Spain from Morocco across the Straits, was called Tarik. He

161

landed near the Rock in 711 A.D., and established a foothold there from which the Moors went on to conquer the rest of Spain and forced their way as far north as Toulouse in central France. They called the Rock *Djebel Tarik* - the Mountain of Tarik - after him. Over the centuries this has been corrupted into *Gibraltar*.'

'Very slowly the Christian princes of northern Spain threw off the Moorish yoke and began the gradual re-conquest of Spain which took some 800 years to complete. They eventually took Gibraltar in 1462, but they held it for only 242 years. The British took it in 1704 and have been there ever since under the terms of the Treaty of Utrecht of 1713, under which it was ceded to the British Crown 'in perpetuity'. That treaty was re-affirmed in five subsequent international treaties, settling European boundaries during the 19th Century.'

'So there is not doubt about Britain's title to the Rock in international law?' guests would interject and I would reply. 'That is undoubtedly so. The British will have been the owners of Gibraltar for almost three centuries. That is longer than the United Kingdom and the United States have existed. The Act of Union was in 1707, and the American Declaration of Independence was in 1776.'

'But what is far more important,' I would continue, 'is that all but about seventy of the original Spanish inhabitants of the Rock fled in 1704 and were gradually replaced by a new people who are not English, nor are they Spanish. They are British Gibraltarians and the Rock is *their* home. They have lived, bred, prospered and suffered great hardship there for those three hundred years, and they have acquired the identity of a people in their own right.'

'But why do they want to be British instead of Spanish Gibraltarians?' Solie might have asked, if she had been able to do so. 'Spain is so much nearer to Gibraltar than England and all the Gibraltarians speak a kind of Spanish.'

'How would you have liked to become an American White just because Mrs Manolsen put you into that basket with them.?' I would have replied. 'We are what the Almighty has made us, and we, humans, have a great affinity for our birth places.'

'The sad thing' I would continue, 'is that the Gibraltarians and Spaniards were good friends from 1807, when Napoleon invaded Spain and we helped the Spanish guerrilla forces to defeat him, until 1954 when Franco started his campaign to get the Rock back on the grounds that it was a British colony on Spanish soil. He claimed that under the United Nations' De-Colonisation Resolutions that Gibraltar should be returned to Spain in order to restore the territorial integrity of the Spanish realm.'

'The British interpretation of those resolutions was totally different. Dependent territories, in the British view, should be de-colonized by handing them back to their indigenous inhabitants. It was for the people of a territory to decide under whose sovereignty, if any, that they wished to live. And so a referendum was held in Gibraltar in 1967 to let the Gibraltarians express their wishes on Sovereignty.

'Only 44 people opted for Spain out of the 12,138 who voted. Britain kept her word and introduced a new Constitution two years later, which gave the Gibraltarians two things: internal self-government and a promise that ran as follows:

'*...Her Majesty's Government will never enter into arrangements under which the people of Gibraltar would pass under the Sovereignty of an other state against their freely and democratically expressed wishes.*

'Franco was furious at this turn of events and slammed the frontier gates shut, hoping to gain his ends by political and economic siege of the Rock. It only made the Gibraltarians more fiercely anti-Spanish. He died in 1975, having failed to recover the Rock. It was now my job, as Governor in the post-Franco era, to help Her Majesty's Government persuade the new Spanish democracy to follow the fundamental democratic principle of honouring the wishes of the people, and to raise the siege as soon as possible.'

One of my difficulties was to find telling analogies to put over the Gibraltarians' case to the many journalists and television teams, who used to descend on the Rock from time to time when the subject of its future was interesting the media. The one that I used most often was inspired by Solie. She was sitting on my desk one stormy day, staring out of the window at the wind whipping spray off the tops of the waves in the Bay although the sun was also shining. She reminded me of Aesop's fable of *The Wind and the Sun*, which I had read as a child.

In Aesop's story, the Wind and the Sun accept a challenge to show which could take a traveller's coat off quickest. The Wind won the toss and tried first. It roared and howled, but the traveller only clutched his cloak all the more tightly to him. The Sun came out and the traveller was more than happy to take off his coat without prompting. Spain has acted like the Wind and forced the Gibraltarians to wrap themselves ever more tightly in the Union Jack. If only the Spaniards would emulate the Sun and become good neighbours again, much of the tension would go out of the situation. The Gibraltarians may not accept Spanish sovereignty, but, at least, the people on both sides of the frontier will be able to help each other in creating economic activity and wealth around the Bay of Gibraltar.

During my time as Governor, Joan and I struggled to put this message across to our many visitors. We felt that Spain's new Government really wanted to be rid of the counter-productive restrictions imposed on Gibraltar by their fascist predecessors. But we knew also that the Spanish and British are proud people. Some face-saving formula was needed by both sides.

A great deal of thought and negotiation went on in London, Madrid and Gibraltar. Just such a formula emerged and was enshrined in the Lisbon Agreement, signed by Lord Carrington and Señor Oreja, the two Foreign Ministers, on April Fools' Day 1980.

The formula was composed like a sandwich with the usual three layers. The bread on the top was a reaffirmation of Spain's historic claim to the Rock; and the bottom slice was Britain's equally clear reiteration of the pledge to respect the freely and democratically expressed wishes of the Gibraltarians. The meat in the middle was Britain's agreement to negotiate on a 'mutually beneficial basis' any proposals that either side wished to raise. Sovereignty was not excluded; nor was it mentioned either. Spain for her part would lift the siege. Negotiations would start simultaneously with the opening of the frontier.

We were all delighted with the compromise that had been reached, and I had visions of going down in Gibraltar's history as the Governor who opened the frontier. Sadly it was not to be. Oreja and his successor, Perez Llorca, failed to persuade their colleagues in the Spanish Cabinet that it was a good deal for both sides. There were still too many Franco men in positions of power and influence in Madrid, who refused to accept the failure of the Spanish ploy to win back the Rock. In their view, anything that the Gibraltarians were prepared to accept, however reluctantly as was the case with the Lisbon Agreement, must be bad for Spain.

The Spanish Government never actually repudiated its Foreign Minister's signature, but 1980 and 1981 passed without a date being fixed for negotiations to begin and for the siege to be lifted.

'I thought that the Spaniards had the reputation of never breaking their word.' Joan remarked one evening when yet one more effort by our ambassador in Madrid came to nothing.

'I believed that too.' I replied. 'But they get so emotional about Gibraltar that they forget their natural good manners and behave atrociously towards the Gibraltarians. They do not seem to realise that if they continue to hector and harass them, they make it impossible for the people of Gibraltar to be polite in return and to sit down and discuss a sensible future that would be of benefit to people on both sides of the frontier.'

One of the problems I discovered when dealing with Spanish diplomats is that we interpret Latin based words which look the same in both languages, quite differently. A particular case in point was the much used word *Negotiation*. To the Spaniard it means finding a way to an objective that has already been decided upon: to us it means finding a compromise that both sides in an argument can accept. There is an ocean of difference between the two as the failure of the Lisbon Agreement demonstrated.

Señor Oreja thought that the negotiations agreed in the Lisbon Agreement were aimed at the return of the Rock to Spain.

165

He used to talk about laying a railway track on which the Gibraltar train could reach its preordained destination of Spanish sovereignty. We saw the negotiations as talks about matters of mutual interest that would bring about the restoration of friendly relations with Spain after the frontier had been opened. We had absolutely no intention of discussing sovereignty or planning its hand over without the consent of the Gibraltarians.

Spanish prevarication was brought to an abrupt halt in January 1982, when Mrs Thatcher confronted their Prime Minister, Calvo Sotelo, during a meeting in Downing Street. She told him bluntly that unless he implemented the Lisbon Agreement, Britain would find it very difficult to support Spain's entry into the E.E.C. as strongly as she would wish. 22nd April was set for the simultaneous opening of the frontier and the start of negotiations. The Portuguese Government agreed that the two sides should meet at a neutral venue at Cintra, just to the north of Lisbon.

When the news reached us in Gibraltar there was some relief, but no undue optimism. An Anglo-Spanish agreement on Gibraltar seemed as unlikely as the ending of bull-fighting in Spain or fox-hunting in England.

'Or until the Barbary Apes desert the Rock.' Solie might have suggested. They were no friends of hers. She knew instinctively that their presence on the Upper Rock was one of the reasons why we did not allow her to go up to the Cottage with us at weekends. We feared that in a scrap with one of them Solie was unlikely to be the winner.

The myth that British sovereignty over the Rock will only end if and when its apes die out or leave, is too well known for repetition in this book about Solie. Paul Gallico's *Scruffy* is a delightful tale about them that I could not hope to better. But he wrote it some years ago against the background of the Second World War, so it is perhaps worth recording briefly the state of the two Ape packs in the early 1980s.

Spanish chances of recovering the Rock look slim if the indicator of Ape fertility is to be taken seriously. They have rarely been more contented and fecund. They regularly exceed their authorised establishment of 36 Apes and Apelets; and each year two or three breeding couples are exported to carefully selected safari parks in Western Europe. The fortunes of the Barbary Apes in the Riff Mountains across the Straits, from which they were brought originally by the Moorish invaders of Spain, are not so rosy. Indeed, there is a danger that they may die out all together there, so it is important that the Rock's two packs should flourish to preserve the species.

In the old days, the apes roamed freely on the Upper Rock, feeding on berries and succulent plants. When food became scarce in winter, they would come down into the city to forage for food in gardens and houses, which was far from popular. And so two feeding points were set up, one for each pack, to keep them away from precious window boxes and clothes lines. They loved eating the best plants out of the former, and could not resist filching brightly coloured garments off the latter!

The Upper Pack lives in seclusion around Middle Hill, the central part of the Rock's razor-back ridge and within the military restricted area around the defence installations sited all along the top of the Rock. It is the special preserve of anthropologists and other scientists, who may wish to study Apes in their natural habitat.

The Lower Pack is more accessible, as it lives around Apes' Den, which was built specially for them on Ferdinand's Battery at the bottom end of Philip II's Wall. It is the 'tourist' pack, who have become inured to a diet of choc-ices, bubble-gum and all the other delights that tourists give them despite the large notices saying, *'Please do not feed the Apes'*.

There has always been a 'Fagin' amongst the Lower Pack, who teaches its youngsters the art of picking pockets and thieving from gullible tourists. The techniques of distracting the victim's attention while other members of the gang steal his possessions is well practised and works to perfection. Necklaces, glasses, earrings, cameras, binoculars, and anything else that shines, are snatched from the unwary and carried off in leaps and bounds up the crags. The victims are left breathless just watching their possessions disappear up the crags. The more inaccessible rocks and undergrowth around Apes' Den are littered with trinkets of all kinds, and with the wing-mirrors, aerials and windscreen-wiper blades snatched from unattended cars!

The health and happiness of both packs rested, in our day, in the capable hands of Sergeant Holmes of the Gibraltar Regiment, who had looked after them for more years than he could remember. He understood them; almost spoke their language; fed them; tended to their medical needs; and sorted out their social problems as far as he could with a rough and ready justice that they seemed to accept.

All Apes and Apelets, male and female, are on the strength of the Gibraltar Regiment, through whose accounts Her Majesty's Government provides money to pay for the feeding and wellbeing of the packs. Every birth and death is duly recorded in Regimental Orders. Newly born Apelets in the Lower Pack are usually named after V.I.P.s. One was named 'William' after me. The C.O. of the Gibraltar Regiment, Colonel Domingo Collado, asked Joan if she would like one named after her? He had to explain, however, that there had been no girls born to the mums of the Lower Pack that year. Would she, he asked, mind giving her name to one of the Upper Pack girls?

Her reply was very swift, 'Certainly not: I would never see her! I would not be able to take an interest in her. I'll wait until next year, thank you!' And she did. There is now a 'Joan' in the Lower Pack.

The total strength of both packs was fixed at 36 by an eminent zoologist some years ago on the grounds that packs of over 18 strong tend to split and form new packs. He seems to have been right as no new packs have formed. This, however, does not mean that peace reigns eternal amongst the Rock's Ape population. The Ape world suffers most of the social problems experienced by the human race. Discipline in each pack is maintained by the leader. Minor crimes are punished by sending the culprit to coventry for varying periods. For more serious crimes, offenders can be outlawed. Murder is not as uncommon as it should be!

Joan one day asked Sergeant Holmes what had happened to the apelets named after our immediate predecessors, Sir John and Lady Cecile Grandy, whose names did not appear on the nominal role. It seems that 'John' was murdered and 'Cecile' died mysteriously. This was nothing to the goings-on during our last year on the Rock. The boys of the Upper Pack cast covetous eyes on some of the nubile girls of the Lower Pack, and proceeded to emulate the rape of the Sabine women! The raid was highly successful and encouraged further aggression. Their deputy leader decided that he was man enough to challenge the leader of the Lower Pack and to usurp his position. He won the ensuing fight that ended with him throwing his rival to his death from the cliff top upon which Apes' Den is built.

It is fun to pretend that the sovereignty of the Rock depends upon the fertility of the Apes, but, as Joan pointed out when we received our annual invitation to the Girl Guides' Thinking Day parade and service, the young people are far more important to Gibraltar's future than any Barbary Apes. We both took a great interest in the Scouts, Guides, Cubs and Brownies, who are enthusiastically supported in Gibraltar.

I asked the Commissioners what we could do to help maintain that enthusiasm in view of the possible opening of the frontier, which might offer so many other counter-attractions. The idea that we came up with was to institute 'the Governor's Troop', on the lines of the Sovereign's Company at Sandhurst. We had a specially ornate staff made by the Dockyard, which was to be carried on parade by the troop that won the annual 'Governor's Scout Troop' competition for it. We presented a silver plate vase for a similar competition amongst the Guides. We also decreed that it should be the Governor's responsibility to set the theme for the year upon which the competitions would be based.

When the time came for me to decide the theme, my mind went blank. Solie came to my rescue as I sat at my desk hoping for inspiration. She provided it. My wastepaper-basket was overflowing and she was scattering the paper over the floor, having a bit of mousing practice.

'That's it,' I said to myself, '"Keep Gibraltar Tidy" will be this year's theme.'

One of the worst things about Gibraltar was, and I believe still is, the rubbish that mars every street, viewing point, historic monument and places of public interest. With a lot of nagging I achieved some temporary improvement, but things always slipped back. It was not the Government Cleansing Department's fault. It was the sheer thoughtlessness of young and old alike, who dropped their litter wherever they happened to be. No one ever thought of putting it into the numerous bins provided for the purpose. The only real solution seemed to be the education of the younger generation, though I had no illusion about the difficulty of putting the message across and making it stick.

On Guides's Thinking Day, all the young people assembled in the Queen's Cinema with their parents. I started my speech setting out the theme for the year with two empty Coca Cola cans on the rostrum so that everyone could see them. My punch line was in two parts:

'Don't....' I said, throwing one can over my shoulder.

Much to my surprise the hall erupted with roars of laughter. I had forgotten that the Guide Colour Parties were drawn up close behind me on the stage. Fortunately the can hit no one: they all ducked just in time.

I doubted afterwards whether many of the children heard the second half of the line even though I did pause for the giggling to die down.

'Put it in the bin', I shouted, dropping the second can with a clang into a dustbin specially placed beside me on the stage.

The message had made a greater impact than I expected. A few days later I was walking down one of the flights of steps that abound in the city, when I heard two young voices calling:

'Governor! Governor! We've done what you said. We've eaten our crisps and we have put the empty packet in the bin!'

The message had after all gone home, but it will take many more years before a generation grows up that is both litter conscious and has the personal discipline to keep Gibraltar tidy. The same, of course, applies to Britain!

CHAPTER 14

TIME FOR HOME

Margaret Thatcher's success in imposing 22nd April upon Calvo Sotello as the date for implementation of the Lisbon Agreement made a great impact upon most peoples' lives in Gibraltar, because they could start planning what they would do once the frontier was open. It also affected Solie's and our lives very materially.

My tour as Governor was due to end in May 1982. My successor, Admiral Sir David Williams, had been selected and was making his arrangements to come out. But a change of Governor just a month after the frontier was opened did not seem a very sensible arrangement, so I was asked to stay on until the end of September. We were then to be taken home in H.M.S. *Invincible*, Britain's newest carrier.

Joan and I were delighted to have an extra four months on the Rock and the chance of visiting Spain. We started planning a celebration trip to Madrid to stay with Richard Parsons, the British Ambassador, who had done so much to bring about the original Lisbon Agreement and to overcome subsequent Spanish prevarication.

Solie was not so pleased. The very thought of going home, whenever it might occur, was abhorrent to her, since it meant six months in quarantine. As she never liked the hot summer months in Gibraltar, and particularly the Levanter, we decided to send her home by air in May so that she would not have too long to wait after we arrived back in October.

When you come to leave a place after some years, you realise that you have not done half the things you had hoped to do. This

172

was very true of Solie. Throughout her four years in the Convent, she had not, as far as we knew, made any lasting cat friendships. Occasionally stray moggies would make their way over the roof tops into the Convent grounds, but she made no attempt to befriend them. On the contrary, she would beat a hasty retreat into our bedroom and call for help. Everything seemed to change after she heard that she was going home in four months' time. She became positively cat-gregarious!

Jeremy Howard's family lived in the Military Assistant's Quarter at the far end of the Convent garden. They took on a very nice black and white kitten, whom their children called 'Puddy'. He came into the garden out of curiosity and Solie visited the Howard house for the same reason. Sadly no real friendship developed, and she seemed to have no desire to mother Puddy. More usually she set about boxing his ears and chasing him home whenever they met, which was a pity because he was a very well behaved kitten and would have made an ideal companion for her.

Much to our disgust she fell madly in love with a buccaneering ginger tom, who could not have been a stray because he had a bright red collar and was in very good condition. The only thing that really worried us about him was how he was getting in and out of the Convent. Clearly he had a secret route, known only to himself. I had seen him in the road outside the Convent so I knew that he was not living rough in the garden. Joan and I feared that he might impart the secret of his route to Solie, and might even seduce her into escaping from the quiet seclusion of the Convent into the riotous freedom of city life.

'Wouldn't it be just like her to elope now that she knows that quarantine lies ahead of her?' Joan remarked.

'She's probably planning to emulate the Grey Lady.' I replied, then feeling a qualm as I said it that many a true word is spoken in jest.

At first we treated 'Ginger', as we called him, as a harmless if unwanted interloper. I tried to trap him several times, but he was far too quick and experienced in evasion for me. I thought that

I had him cornered one night in the drawing-room. I shut the doors quickly and asked the duty footman to call the RSPCA inspector to remove him. When we opened the doors about half an hour later, he had gone! I could swear that there were no windows open when I trapped him, but we found that one was ajar when we looked round for his escape route. He must have pawed it open in the same way that we knew Solie could do when she was so minded.

Then one night I heard 'Ginger' calling Solie. I looked out of our bedroom window and saw them playing happily together beside the patio fountain. I did not have the heart to break up their platonic friendship. She was, after all, neuter any way, and I suspect that he was too. Knowing that she would be off to her quarantine cattery all too soon, I left them alone.

We did, however, draw the line a few weeks later, when Solie invited Ginger up to share her supper, which was always set up in Joan's bathroom, next to our bedroom. The silly fellow would talk and woke us up! I vowed that I would catch him, but he was always far too nimble for me. We never did discover who owned him.

One of the most exciting events in Gibraltar's annual calender was the arrival of the Fleet for the 'Spring Train' naval exercises in the sea areas around the Rock. At the beginning of April 1982, the harbour was filled with some twenty-five British warships and half a dozen submarines, two of which were nuclear. Some 5,000 sailors and marines came ashore, and were hosted by the Staffords and the R.A.F. at North Front as well as the naval shore establishment, H.M.S. *Rooke* and the inhabitants of city and pubs of Gibraltar. The Convent had a full complement of senior naval officers and their wives, who had flown out from England for this annual naval occasion.

At Guard Mounting that week the Staffords' band-master decided to put on a special display of drumming for the Fleet's benefit. Solie had not been warned and was sitting in her usual place in the balcony room, when they started their brilliant but noisy performance. Later Solie was nowhere to be found. She did not attend the dinner party that night, and had not reappeared when we went to bed. There was a full moon so I suggested to Joan that she was probably out with Ginger and she should not worry.

At about four in the morning we were woken by the fiendish din of a cat fight on the bastion below our windows. Joan was sure that Solie was involved and was being set upon by the bastion strays. Knowing that there would be no sleep until Solie was back, and fearing that Joan might be right, I struggled into my dressing-gown and set off with a torch to see what could be done. I asked one of the Convent policemen on night-duty to help me search the garden and the bastion.

Our search revealed nothing, other than a couple of sailors enjoying the favours of local girls in the privacy of the old gun emplacements. On my way back to our suite, I kept to the grass rather than walking on the gravel paths so that I could hear any faint cries for help. Sure enough, as I approached our wing, I did hear something that I thought might be Solie. Our torches revealed nothing in the bougainvillaea and other creepers on the walls, but I could still hear snatches of something that might be Solie in trouble. The sound seemed to change direction and pitch as if the source was moving about quite fast.

The policeman was the first to realise where Solie was.

'Sir! the roof,' he called shining his torch onto the balustrade above our bedroom. We just caught a momentary glimpse of a pair of bright eyes in the beam. I rushed up the backstairs and tried the door onto the roof, which I had ordered should always be kept locked after the previous episode over the billiard room. It was shut but *not* locked. When I opened it a very hoarse, tired and angry Solie rushed past me down to her feeding bowls in Joan's bathroom.

Piecing events together at breakfast next morning, we concluded that, after being frightened by the Staffords' drummers, she had rushed away and happened to find the roof door open as some of our guests were up there watching ships of the Fleet entering harbour. They had not noticed her, and had shut, but not locked, the door when they came down into the house again. The handle was too high for Solie to do her door opening trick.

All's well that ends well, and it was perhaps a good thing that we did not know that we were about to experience our most exciting and difficult time in Gibraltar. On the day after what was to prove to be our last major Solie hunt, Admiral Sandy Woodward, flying his flag in H.M.S. *Glamorgan*, arrived with the last Spring Train ships. Gibraltar had had a happy and relatively trouble free few days entertaining the earlier arrivals. I noticed how much more modern the ships looked. Three of the latest frigates, *Broad Sword*, *Battle Axe*, and *Brilliant* were present. Amongst the County Class destroyers were *Sheffield*, *Plymouth*, *Coventry*, and the Type 22 frigates included *Ardent* and *Antelope*. There were comparatively few of the Navy's old work-horses, the Leander Class frigates, which were being phased out of service, like our beloved *Apollo* that was eventually sold to the Pakistan navy.

Admiral Sir John Fieldhouse, C-in-C Fleet, and his wife 'Midge', arrived to stay a few days with us in the Convent while the exercises were in progress. Their stay was to be cut short dramatically. We were all assembled for dinner in the drawing-room when my ADC, then Chris Sexton, came in with a 'Flash' signal, which I handed straight to the Admiral. The Falklands had been invaded by Argentina!

The Spring Train exercises stopped abruptly as the Fleet prepared to meet reality. Half the ships were ordered to sail southwards to Ascension Island as soon as they had taken on board all the ammunition, stores and supplies that they needed from the Rock's depots and from the other half of the ships, which were detailed to return to England. Within hours, R.A.F. *Hercules* transports were arriving at North Front to refuel on their way south to start the establishment of an advanced base at Ascension.

The Falklands are 7,000 miles from Gibraltar, but the political parallels between the Argentinian claim to the islands and the Spanish claim to the Rock were too close for comfort. A few days later, I flew back to London for consultations. In one of the Foreign Office corridors I met Rex Hunt, the Governor of the Falklands, who had just got back.

'You next!' he said, pointing a finger at me. All Gibraltar, including Joan and Solie, thought so too!

Successful aggression can be catching. It would not take much to inspire one of the Provincial Captains General in Spain to try making his name by attacking the Rock. He would certainly become Spain's greatest hero if he were to succeed in capturing it.

We were, indeed, the next, but in rather a different way. The Argentine invasion of the Falklands, and Britain's reaction to it, gave the Spanish Government the pretext for, at least temporarily, suspending the Lisbon Agreement, which they had never liked. Lord Carrington resigned over the Falklands crisis and so we had no Foreign Secretary with whom they could open negotiations. In any case, they claimed, public opinion in Spain would not accept the opening of the Gibraltar frontier while Britain was at war with their Argentinian cousins. There was little that the Foreign Office could do but accept a postponement until 25th June, by which time it was hoped matters in the Falklands would be settled one way or another.

For the next few weeks Gibraltar put itself onto a war footing. Everyone did his or her best to help the Fleet and to bring the Rock's defences up to a high state of alert. We were sure that the Spanish Government would not countenance any attack on Gibraltar, but we could not be certain that there was not a potential El Cid or Don Quixote amongst the Spanish military, whom no one trusted after their recent attempted coup when the Spanish Parliament was held at gun point in full view of the television cameras.

Gibraltar's greatest feat was the conversion of the cruise ship *Uganda* into a hospital ship over one short weekend. She arrived on a Friday evening in the black and white British India Line colours. She left on Monday morning gleaming white with huge Red Crosses on her hull and funnel, and a new helicopter-landing deck constructed over her stern. Inside, operating theatres had been set up and wards equipped; and doctors and nurses, flown out from England, were getting the ship properly organised. As she sailed away that morning, all Gibraltar turned out to wave her farewell. There were lumps in many throats and tears in many eyes.

Nowhere in the British Commonwealth, including Britain herself, were the losses suffered by the Task Force felt more keenly than in Gibraltar. Spanish radio and television, which are listened to and watched on the Rock, poured out the Argentinian version of events, however tendentious and fanciful, without giving anything of the British side of the story. The people of Gibraltar, however, heard the British media's account of events as well, and as they did so anti-Spanish sentiment grew in intensity.

Gibraltarian morale rose and fell with events in the South Atlantic. Joy at the recapture of South Georgia and the sinking of the *Belgrano* was soon offset by the news of the successful Exocet attack on H.M.S. *Sheffield*, which was so well known in Gibraltar that her loss seemed very personal. Spirits rose again with the landings at Carlos Bay, but the agony returned with the loss of *Ardent, Antelope* and *Coventry,* all of which had been in Gibraltar so recently for Spring Train. The capture of Darwin by 2nd Parachute Battalion was soon overshadowed by the disaster at Bluff Cove, an event that was accompanied by the most outrageous fabrications by the Spanish media.

The two British carriers, *Invincible* and *Hermes* were sunk over and over again in Spanish news bulletins. But when Argentinian resistance suddenly collapsed at Port Stanley, the Spanish television news readers could not look their audiences in the face. They read their scripts without looking up.

In Gibraltar there was a spontaneous outburst of suppressed emotion. Every building was decorated with Union Jacks and garlanded with the red, white, and blue bunting used for the Prince and Princess of Wales's honeymoon visit. Of their own volition, and before anything similar had been started in Britain, the Gibraltarians began their own British Task Force Fund, which soon raised £63,000 from street collections and personal contributions. This figure did not include major contributions by the Government and commercial firms, or the value of the free holidays given to many of the wounded during their convalescence by the Rock's hoteliers. It was a stirring effort. The tax-paying population is only 12,000 strong.

One of the main losers from the conflict was loyal Gibraltar. The Spanish Government lost its nerve again and asked for the indefinite postponement of the frontier opening. They could quite justifiably claim that public opinion in Spain was too inflamed by the events in the South Atlantic to make the implementation of the Lisbon Agreement a politically practicable proposition. It would, indeed, have looked too like another Latin humiliation at the hands of the Anglo-Saxons for any Spanish Government to contemplate.

For a few weeks it looked as if Joan and I would be asked to stay on for another year to help Gibraltar over the difficult period that we all could see lay ahead with the continuation of the siege and anti-British feeling running so high in Spain. Both major political parties and the Chamber of Commerce wanted me to stay on, and the various women's associations wanted Joan to do so too. A press campaign was mounted in Gibraltar, but both Joan and I agreed with the Foreign Office view that now was the time to go. The Lisbon Agreement was as near dead as made no matter. Its revival or replacement would take far longer than a year to accomplish, and so our date of departure was left as the end of September.

We had delayed Solie's return to England while the Argentinian crisis was unresolved, but there was now no excuse for further delay. We booked her into the Quarantine Cattery and bought her ticket home on British Airways. I had already promised Joan that I would see to her embarkation, and so on the appointed day I whisked her into her travelling cat basket and sealed the wire grill. Into the Daimler she went, protesting that she had not been allowed to say goodbye to Ginger or to any of her many other friends in the Convent.

179

Solie wailed all the way to the airport in that pitiful complaining voice that only Siamese can make. The last that I saw of her until we ourselves got back to England was her face looking out of the basket as it was loaded into the rear compartment of a Boeing 737. As the doors closed, Solie's days as the Governor's cat closed too.

In the first five years of her life she had been:

Solo;

Solo, the Governor's Cat (Designate);

Solie, the Governor's Cat;

and now she was about to become Solo again, the Governor's Cat (Retired) and mistress of West Stowell.

CHAPTER 15

FAREWELL TO THE ROCK

Solie's quick and unapplauded return to England in the baggage compartment at the back of a Boeing 737, confined in her cat basket, was diametrically the opposite to our journey home. H.M.S. *Invincible* was no longer available to take us back as she was still in the South Atlantic. Admiral Fieldhouse, however, arranged for us to depart in the assault ship *Fearless*, also of Falklands fame. She was setting out on a Mediterranean training cruise for midshipmen and would be in Gibraltar on 4th October. Instead of sailing straight home to England, we would land at Naples and have a fortnight's holiday on the Sorrento Peninsular before flying home.

Poor Solo had not been so lucky. She had been petrified by her flight home in that noisy luggage compartment, and refused to eat when she reached Mr Turner's quarantine cattery at Sherlock Row, near Reading. Fortunately Joan flew home soon afterwards for the birth of our second grandchild. She rang Mr Turner up as soon as she was back at West Stowell. He was very worried about her, and was contemplating force feeding her. Although he did not usually like owners to visit until their cats had settled down to their new routine, he asked Joan to come over straight away.

Joan's visit had a miraculous effect. Solo knew that she had not been deserted by her own family and voluntarily agreed to take a little food from her. The crisis was over, but for the next few weeks Solo would only eat at night. She was rarely seen out of her hutch in daylight, and she would never join the other inmates in singing 'Oh! Why are we waiting...' at meal times. It took her a good month to realise that she was no longer the

Governor's Cat, and to settle down to her new life as one of Mr Turner's guests.

As August faded into September, and as the heat and humidity of a persistent Levanter eased, our lives became almost as nocturnal as Solo's. People of all walks of life wanted to say goodbye by entertaining us in one way or another. The spectrum of events ranged from an informal 'get together' with the old people of the Senior Citizens' Club to the magnificent farewell dinner given to us by the Speaker of the House of Assembly. We were rarely in bed during that last month before midnight.

We were particularly touched by a public subscription organised by the Editor of *Panorama*, Joe Garcia, and Major Momy Levy, who always attended Guard Mounting so regularly every week, to present us with a beautifully carved model in Gibraltar stone of the Convent balcony with its two flags flying. We could only accept it on trust. It will be returned to the Gibraltar Museum when our days are over.

During that last month I had to make innumerable speeches. I missed the inspiration that Solo provided as she sat on my desk staring pensively out of the study window. Some of the themes that she might have suggested jostled in my mind:

'The people of Gibraltar are no more Spanish or English than Solo is an American White. They are British Gibraltarians and the Rock is *their* home......'

'The wishes of the Gibraltarians about their future are just as important as those of the British colonists in North America, who drafted the Declaration of Independence in 1776, seventy-two years after the Rock was taken by Admiral Rooke.......'

'There can be no constructive solution to the vexed Gibraltar question until Spain accepts that the wishes as well as the interests of the Gibraltarians are paramount in deciding the Rock's future......'

'Hopefully, Spain's desire to become a truly Western democracy will lead, in the end, to her becoming a good neighbour to Gibraltar......'

'On the one hand, there is the right of a small nation to its home, where it has lived, bred, prospered and often suffered severe hardships for almost three centuries; and on the other, there is the emotional craving of a large European state for the restoration of its territorial integrity through the return of an ancient fortress that it once possessed for a shorter time than it has been the home of the British Gibraltarians.....'

I could not resist emphasizing, whenever I spoke, how petty it was for a nation of 36 million people to go on coercing a mere 20,000 Gibraltarians, who had made it abundantly clear through their long and steadfast resistance to the 15th Siege of the Rock that they had no wish to be absorbed into the Spanish realm.

I was never prepared to predict when the golden age of Hispano-Gibraltarian good-neighbourliness would dawn. I had been proved over-optimistic too often during my days as Governor. I did, however, promise that Joan, Solo and I would keep in close touch with events in Gibraltar when we were back in West Stowell. The frontier was grudgingly opened in 1985, and there has been preciously little sign of good-neighbourliness in Madrid since then.

4th October came all too soon. It was a Monday so we had one last weekend up at the cottage and on the barge. The former was a success, but the latter was not. I caught nothing, but since Solie was not waiting in the Convent for her fresh fish supper only my pride as a fisherman was hurt!

As with all Monday mornings, we started off with Guard Mounting at 10.30 a.m., but this time it was a very special and poignant parade. The Convent Square was filled to overflowing, not with tourists, but with Gibraltarian well-wishers, who had come to say farewell. Some of the tiny tots from the primary schools were holding up cards with letters on them, spelling out 'Goodbye'. The Staffords' band played our favourite tunes; their Corps of Drums carried out the drumming display that had scared Solie out of her wits; and their trumpeters and buglers played a specially composed farewell fanfare, leading into the National Anthem. The Old Guard marched off to the strains of *Auld Lang*

Syne. There were few dry eyes on the Convent balcony or in the crowd below.

A quick change out of uniform, and Joan and I were in the gallery of the Supreme Court to watch the annual opening of the new legal year by the Chief Justice. Afterwards we had an opportunity to say goodbye to the members of the Bar at a cocktail party before returning to the Convent for a quick informal lunch with our personal staff. Then back into full ceremonial dress for the last time in Gibraltar, but regrettably without Solie to assist. Fleet Chief rose to the occasion by arriving in our suite with a bottle of champagne from the staff to reinforce our morale for our actual departure.

As we came out of the front door of the Convent for the last time, we found the square packed again. This time representative contingents from all the voluntary organisations and charities, with which Joan was associated, were in the front of the crowd. The Guard of Honour was from the Gibraltar Regiment with its Colours and fifes and drums. The National Anthem crashed out for the penultimate Royal Salute of our departure. After inspecting the Guard of Honour, Joan and I went round the square shaking as many hands as we could before getting into the Daimler for our drive to the Dockyard where *Fearless* was berthed.

Something seemed to be missing. Both Fleet Chief and I realised simultaneously what it was: no Keys! There was an awkward pause while he rushed up to the dining-room to fetch them and to hand them to me for the last time as he had done so often before the ceremony of the Keys.

Main Street was packed with school children and those people who could not get into the Convent Square to wish us farewell. We were soon down in the Dockyard with the grey bulk of *Fearless* towering above us. I mounted the dais to return the Royal Salute of the three Services' Guards of Honour, holding the Keys aloft for the last time.

Our departure was the reverse of our arrival with one very special exception. We shook hands with the long line of V.I.P.s, stretching to the foot of *Fearless*'s brow, finally saying goodbye to

Sir Joshua and Lady Hassan. I had worked so closely with him over our four and a half years on the Rock that it was appropriate that the Chief Minister, as the elected representative of the people of Gibraltar, should, on this occasion, take precedence over the Chief Justice, who was very happy to accept this momentary demotion.

I had one last and final duty to perform before starting to climb the brow. The Escort to the Keys was marched forward with R.S.M. Saunders, the Port Sergeant, at their head. He halted in front of me and saluted. I thrust the Keys out to him with even a greater clatter than usual, saying:

'Make sure the Fortress is kept secure, Port Sergeant!'

'We, *all*, will, Sir!' was his impromptu reply.

As soon as we reached the top of *Fearless*'s steep brow, it was lifted off by a dock-side crane and she started to edge away from the quay. The band of the Staffords on shore and the band of my own Corps, the Royal Engineers, on board, played us away. Out of every corner of the harbour came flotillas of small boats intent on escorting us to sea and waving us farewell. In one of the launches were half a dozen or so lawyers still in their court-room rig. They pursued us, waving champagne bottles and glasses, and were soaked by *Fearless*'s wake as she gathered speed. They did not care: they had just rushed down from the Bar lunch, marking the beginning of the new Legal Year - what did a bit of sea water matter?

Captain Jeremy Larken, who was in command of *Fearless* during the South Atlantic Campaign and had been awarded a DSO for gallantry, took her close inshore the whole way round the Rock until we reached Catalan Bay before turning eastwards into the Mediterranean where we were joined by our two escort frigates and a Fleet supply-ship, which were to sail with us to Naples.

By then the light was beginning to fade. Our last recollection of Gibraltar will always be the sound of the church bells of Catalan Village peeling out across the water with the stark rugged silhouette of the Rock fading from sight as the dusk engulfed us as we watched from *Fearless*'s bridge.

CHAPTER 16

SOLO, THE GOVERNOR'S CAT
(RETIRED)

Our's and Solo's days of overseas postings were over. We all wondered how we and she should face retirement. Many people had warned us that we would find ourselves busier than ever. I had my doubts as I put my general officer's sword away into the glass fronted cabinet in the drawing-room. There was the garden to help keep me busy, and with no staff available any more I accepted a division of duties with Joan: I would do all the unskilled chores, leaving her free to use her expertise in the more exacting tasks in the kitchen and about the house.

Solo took to retirement with evident glee. She arrived out of the quarantine cattery in high spirits. We thought that she might have forgotten West Stowell after her five years away, but not a bit of it. We soon heard the cat-flap slapping and closing as she went to and fro, restoring discipline amongst the denizens of her garden domains. What I think she enjoyed most was the absence of army-booted footmen, hoover-wielding maids, knife-brandishing cooks, blue coated security policemen and all the other people who used to frighten her in the Convent.

It was not long before she reacquired her hunting skills, which had suffered from lack of practice in Gibraltar. She never again achieved her earlier feat of bringing a pigeon in through the cat-flap, but most creatures of slightly lesser size were presented to Joan as tributes of esteem for her mistress.

I was soon in her bad books again because I would try to intercept her and remove her offerings from her before she reached the bedroom. Mice were soon being eaten again behind

Joan's dressing-table, but she still did not like eating shrews. The worst mistake that I could make was to catch her in the midst of a session of shrew-baiting before the shrew had died of shock or exhaustion. If I was foolish enough to do so, shrew-baiting would turn quickly into hunt-the-shrew with Solo and I competing for the prize.

Three particular incidents are engraved in our memories of the first months back at West Stowell. We called them the bat, the moorhen and the water-vole crises.

The bat crisis started in the early hours of one morning before it was light. Joan woke me and said that there was something going on in the bedroom. I switched on the lights and saw Solo sitting on the end of our bed with her head swinging to and fro as if she was watching a tennis match. Joan screamed and shot under the bed-clothes. All I heard was:

'It's a bat!' as she dived for cover.

Sure enough there was a bat circling the high ceiling with Solo proudly watching it and claiming credit for the entertainment potential of her catch! The solution in this case was simple: I just opened the large sash-windows as wide as they would go and switched off the light. I just caught a glimpse of the bat as it sped out to freedom. I heard Solo mutter 'Spoil-sport' as we settled down again to enjoy what was left of the night.

The moorhen saga started in much the same way, but this time when I switched the light on we saw Solo was conducting a rodeo, pursuing a largish bird, which was scuttling - as moorhens do - around the bedroom floor. Foolishly I tried to compete with Solo in catching the moorhen, which only resulted in a triangular contest between the three of us. Then I changed tactics: I lunged for Solo, caught her, and incarcerated her in the bathroom while I tried to catch the moorhen.

Seizing a large bath-towel, I did manage to catch it without much further ado. I carried it off down to the lake, feeling a bit foolish in my pyjamas and dressing gown in the grey light of dawn. As I let Solo's prize catch go, it ran screaming into the water and flapping across the lake to the island and safety. Its cries were taken up by the other resident moorhens:

'Where have you been? Where have you been?' they seemed to be shrieking.

Both the bat and moorhen incidents had been amusing, but the water-vole episode was not such fun. This time we were woken up by a crunching noise and a most appalling smell. I knew that Solo must be filleting and eating something in her butcher's shop/restaurant behind Joan's dressing-table. Sure enough, there she was devouring a huge water-vole from the lake. We had never smelt anything so repulsive! There was no Grand National round the bedroom this time: just clearing away the corpse and blood-stained mess around it - not my idea of fun in the middle of the night! Even after shampooing the carpet several times the smell lingered for days. It was a very angry retired governor who imprisoned his cat in the utility-room for some hours with only hard washing machines, ironing boards and so forth for comfort and no food. There was no question of my being considered by Solo anything so mild as a spoil-sport this time.

Things began to improve after the water-vole incident. Solo became more discerning about what she brought in as presents for Joan, and she decided never to bring in anything worth eating otherwise I would remove it. She set up her own dining parlour - Beatrix Potter fashion - behind the large yew trees just outside our kitchen windows. I accepted this as a very reasonable arrangement, and we were friends again!

Just as we had been warned, I became busier than I had ever been. I rejoined the Cabinet Office Historical Section to complete the last three volumes of the Official Histories of the Second World War; I took on shadow writing and book reviewing for *The Times*; and I agreed with my publishers to write another book. My sword was, indeed, replaced by my pen, and it, in turn, was exchanged for two word-processors and a fax machine.

One of my commissions was to write a series of articles on Maritime versus Continental strategy. Who better to consult on such a subject than Admiral of the Fleet Lord Fieldhouse, the victor of the Falklands Campaign and our guest in the Convent at the start of that exciting time. The Fieldhouses very kindly invited us to lunch at their official flat in Admiralty Arch - he was the First Sea Lord at the time. Joan went in while I parked our car. In the drawing-room she was greeted by two delightful wire-haired dachshunds, just like our old Strudel, who had died just before we moved to West Stowell in 1977.

'Watch Bill's face when he sees these two little people!' Joan said to Midge - Lady Fieldhouse: 'He's besotted with "Wires", especially miniatures.'

Sure enough, I fell for them as soon as I saw them. They were just right: full of enthusiasm and great characters. Midge gave us the address of their breeder, Sheila Palmer, who lived in West Sussex. On our way home, Joan looked across at me and said:

'You'd love one of those wouldn't you?'

I agreed that since we were no longer faced with the quarantine problem there was nothing that I would like better.

'Then I'll give you one for your birthday. You gave me Solo before we went out to Gib, so now its my turn.'

Suddenly she had second thoughts:

'Oh! What about Solo? How will she take to sharing us with a puppy? She's pretty set in her ways.'

'She'll get used to the idea.' I said, trying to disguise my lack of confidence. 'The puppy will be very small. She must have some maternal instincts left. She'll probably want to mother it, I expect.'

A few days later we set off in the car for West Sussex.

Sheila Palmer had given us directions to her farm, which she said was 'in the back of beyond'. It certainly was. When we did find it, we had to make our way up a long farm track through sheep, cows, a few ponies and finally a gaggle of geese near the front door, out of which came a stream of dogs of various sizes, ages and breeds to greet us. Sheila brought up the rear and introduced herself and her dogs, amongst whom there were three 'Wires': a senior bitch called 'Auntie', then Bess, the mother of the latest litter, and behind her trotted the last of her puppies, called Peanut, for whom Sheila was still looking for a home.

Peanut lived up to her name. She was petite, golden, affectionate and very lively with a small question mark curl of darker hair in the middle of her forehead, making her attractively quizzical. Like Solo when I first saw her, I knew Peanut was for me, and she thought so too. The deal was soon struck, and we set off back to West Stowell with little Peanut curled up on Joan's lap, not the least concerned about leaving Bess and her other friends behind. Occasionally she would wake up and give Joan's hand an affectionate lick with her small soft tongue.

During the journey home we discussed Peanut's name. Although it was a most appropriate kennel name and suited her, we could hardly go calling for her with 'Pea, Pea, Pea...', could we?

'She ought to have a German girl's name.' Joan thought: 'Dachshunds were originally German dogs after all'.

Our previous Dachsie, Strudel, had been in a litter of three with kennel names: Apfel Strudel, Wiener Schnitzel, and Pretzel. Apfel Strudel came to us. We just dropped the Apfel, and she became Strudel for the seventeen years of her life. Dropping Pea from Peanut, would have turned my latest girl friend into 'Nutty', which I could not accept. In my eyes she was already highly intelligent!

'Why not Trudie?' Joan suggested.

'That's it!' I replied and Peanut became Trudie almost at once, although I found it difficult at first not to call her Strudie, as they were so alike in colour and temperament.

As we approached West Stowell, we started to worry about Solo's probably adverse reaction to the newest member of our family. our fears were well founded. Solo took Trudie's arrival as an insult and an invasion of her privacy. She made her views quite plain by walking away, and seeking peace and quiet elsewhere whenever Trudie appeared. For three days, a state of armed neutrality, if not war, existed between the two of them. Trudie wanted to play with Solo, but Solo was the spoil-sport this time. She would fizz, arch her back and fuzz out her tail in a most unmotherly way, and Trudie would beat a hasty retreat, wondering what she had done wrong.

On the fourth day, Solo clearly decided that she must exert her seniority in the household and put the little upstart in her place. I had taken up Joan's early morning glass of grapefruit juice to the bedroom, and I had picked up Trudie and put her on the bed while we watched the breakfast television news. Trudie was snuggled down on the eiderdown very content with life, when Solo, who believed that only she should share our bed with us, arrived and jumped up. Before we knew what was happening, there was an ear-piercing yell from Trudie. She had been swiped across the bottom by Solo with her claws out, and a small trickle of blood appeared from where the blow had struck. From that moment onwards it was quite clear who was mistress. Solo might be a retired Governor's cat, but she was not retired in the animal world of West Stowell.

Solo and Trudie have grown to tolerate each other, but they have not become great friends. Trudie and I, however, have become inseparable, and so willy-nilly she became firmly my dog and Solo adamantly Joan's cat. I would hear Joan warning Trudie not to press her luck too far:

'Leave my Solo alone Trudie! You'll get your nose scratched, and what will your master say then?'

As Trudie grew bigger, she and I used to go for longer and longer walks over the Downs behind West Stowell. There were plenty of rabbits and hares to chase, and she was in her seventh heaven when she put up a deer. She would chase it for miles, giving me all the exercise that I needed, trying to keep her in sight. I felt, nevertheless, that what she really needed was a companion with whom she could hunt, and who would give her the companionship that Solo was not prepared to provide.

The days soon came when Trudie was old enough to have puppies, and so we decided that she should be allowed to have at least one family of her own whatever Solo might think about such a proposition. She was successfully mated with a very nice brindle dog, recommended by Sheila Palmer, but sadly things went wrong and she had to have a hysterectomy. Even Solo was sad about it, and she did her very best to help in nursing Trudie back to health.

We had intended to keep one of Trudie's puppies as the companion that I thought she needed, and to find good homes for the rest. Quite by chance Sheila Palmer rang up one night soon after Trudie had lost her pups to say that Bess had just had another litter, and to ask whether we knew of anyone looking for a 'Wire'. I heard Joan ask Sheila to wait an moment while she called me to the phone.

'Would you like one?' she asked, putting her hand over the receiver.

It was as if my and Trudie's prayers had been answered. And so it was that we set off a few days later for Littlehampton, where Sheila now lived, having sold her Sussex farm. The house was easier to find. There were no farm animals around, but her house was just as full of dogs and one very brave cat! Bess was feeding her litter when we arrived so Sheila gave us some coffee while we waited to see her pups. Then Sheila brought in the only 'red' bitch in the litter, thinking that as Trudie was a 'red' we would like to have another puppy that colour, which for anyone other than canine experts is better described as 'gold'.

The little bundle of golden fur that Sheila handed to me was charming in every way but one: she did not take to me as Trudie had done, and I did not take to her either! I do not know why we were incompatible at first sight. She had a rather a snub nose and lacked the innocent enthusiasm that Trudie had shown when we first met. My instincts told me that she would not get on with me, Trudie or Solo.

Sheila sensed my doubts.

'Bess has one other bitch, but she's dark brindle. I have tentatively offered her to someone else, thinking that you would want a red, but I know that the people concerned would prefer her. They would be delighted if you chose the brindle.'

Off Sheila went and came back with Bess and her brindle daughter trotting behind her. I picked the little person up and knew she was for me. She was almost black with eyes sparkling with enthusiasm and an attractively serious expression on her small face as she surveyed me. A quick lick on my nose told me that she had accepted me too. There was only one snag to our whirlwind romance: she would not be old enough to leave Bess for a few weeks. Sheila agreed to bring her to us at West Stowell as soon as she was weaned and ready to start her new life with Trudie and Solo.

It was a lovely summer day when Sheila arrived for lunch at West Stowell. She had brought all her dogs with her for an outing, and to say farewell to Bess's brindle daughter, whom Joan and I had already decided to call Heidi - quite why I can't remember except that it was again a German name. They all trooped into our garden. Solo took one look and dashed for sanctuary in Joan's bedroom.

When lunch was over and it was time for Sheila and her menagerie to depart, I picked up my new little girl friend and cuddled her in my arms as her mother and relations scrambled back into Sheila's car for their return journey. As soon as the car had disappeared down the drive, I put Heidi down on the lawn, wondering what Trudie and Solo would say when they realised that she had not been left behind by mistake and was staying on as a new member of our household.

Trudie was sweet. She wagged her tail and went over to welcome the little scrap to West Stowell. I am sure that she thought Heidi was one of the puppies that she had never had. All her motherly instincts welled up as she tried to make Heidi feel at home. The affection seemed to be mutual. Heidi skipped after her as Trudie showed her round. They have been the firmest friends ever since, sharing everything except bones. Jealousy over bones is one of the few things that can cause them to fall out, but only temporarily.

Solo re-emerged when Sheila's pack had left. She was suspicious of Heidi at first, but she was only rude to her if Heidi came too close. She had a few maternal instincts left and seemed to want to help mothering the new arrival but it was an arm's length relationship as it had been with Trudie. If she was alone with Heidi, the two of them would play in a rather guarded fashion, but, if Trudie joined in, that was just too much for Solo. Her anti-dog instincts got the better of any maternal desires: two dogs ganging up on her was unfair. Off she would dash to Joan's bed, which was too high for 'Tru and Hi', as they became known, to reach her.

As Heidi grew up, walks over the downs and through the woods around West Stowell again grew longer and longer, and I grew fitter and fitter. Tru found hunting with Hi the greatest fun. As soon as I lifted them out of the car at the start of a walk, they would dash off rather like a couple of school-girls hand in hand. They took me up and down steep hill sides, along narrow sheep tracks and through bramble strewn woods in whatever direction their noses told there was something worth chasing. They rarely caught anything, but they and I thoroughly enjoyed our afternoon walks whatever the weather.

Until we had two dogs in the family, I did not realise how distinct their personalities could be. In the case of Tru and Hi, their characters were as different as their colours. Tru was gold, emotional and a very faithful one man dog, who never barked unnecessarily. Hi was silver grey, gregarious and always enthusiastic about anyone she had ever met before. She would go off like a Chinese fire-cracker at the slightest sound, but it was rarely possible to detect from the tone of her barking whether she was greeting friends or repelling boarders! And yet paradoxically, she was a very serious minded little dog, often wearing that worried expression on her small face as she had done when we first met. It was perhaps to tell us that she really did feel just as deeply about things as her more mature and reserved half-sister, Tru.

Together they are a great team. They vie with each other as to who can give friends they know - like the postmen - the loudest and longest welcome; or people they do not know the fiercest barrage of doggy abuse that they can muster. Our local policeman, PC Lewis, says that they are the best burglar-alarms in the district as long as you cannot see how small and friendly they are.

The loudest reception is reserved for me when I get back in the evening after a day in London. Joan brings them down in the car to meet me at Pewsey station. As the train pulls in, they are up at the windows ready to give me what we call their version of a twenty-one gun salute. As I get into the car bedlam breaks out and I am licked all over by two very excited little people. It is almost worth going away for the day just to receive their 'welcome back' salute.

Solo is less demonstrative when I return home, as if to say:

'Its nice to see you back, but do remember I'm her cat. You have those noisy dogs to look after you.'

In the evenings at West Stowell, the whole family are together. While we watch television, Solo takes over Joan's knee, and the two dogs settle on the sofa with me. Retirement is very pleasant when you have enough to do and four girls to look after you - Joan, Solo, Tru and Hi!

Solo agrees. She is now fifteen as I end this story of her life so far. She does not look a day older than she did when she was the Governor's Cat in the Convent. She is, of course, slower and wiser, in that we have fewer mice, voles and other cat delicacies brought into the house. But she too is enjoying her retirement from the duties of Governor's Cat with Tru and Hi to keep her young.

INDEX

198

Other books published by Gibraltar Books Ltd

The Rock of the Gibraltarians: A History of Gibraltar
  by General Sir William G F Jackson
The most up-to date history of Gibraltar by a leading military historian,
with 16 maps, 30 line drawings and 39 photographs.
2nd edition paperback
ISBN 0 948466 14 6   £11.95

**The Fortress Came First: The Evacuation of the Civilian
population of Gibraltar in World War II**
  by Thomas J Finlayson
An in-depth study by the Gibraltar Government Archivist with 72
photographs.
Casebound
ISBN 0 948466 12 X   £14.95

The Western Sephardim: Sephardi Heritage volume II
  Edited by Dr Richard Barnett and Walter Schwab
The history of a number of communities established by Jews exiled
from Spain in 1492.
Casebound
ISBN 0 948466 11 1   £35.00

Centreport Gibraltar
  by A A and D M Sloma assisted by S Johnson
A guide to sailing in the Strait of Gibraltar with plans of the harbour in
the area and along the west coast of Morocco.   With folding charts of
the Strait and the west coast of Morocco.
Spiralbound
ISBN 0 948466 06 5   £16.95

The Birds of Gibraltar
   by J E Cortés, J C Finlayson, M A Mosquera and E F J Garcia
A valuable study of the bird life and migration patterns in this
ornithologically strategic area.
Paperback
ISBN 0 948466 00 6   £4.95

The Guns and Towers of Gibraltar
   by George Palao
A study of the development of the Moorish Castle and other features
of the fortifications of Gibraltar, and the ordnance employed in the
batteries during the last three centuries.
Original paperback
ISBN 0 948466 01 4   £2.95

Sherlock Holmes in Gibraltar
   by Sam Benady
Two short stories in the manner of the master story teller. Is this really
the true story of the *Mary Celeste*?
Original paperback fiction
ISBN 0 948466 15 4   £2.95

The Sale of Gibraltar in 1474
   by Diego Lamelas
An original monograph on a unique and hitherto unknown episode in
the history of Gibraltar. Translated from the Spanish by Sam Benady.
Paperback Original
ISBN 0 948466 20 0   £4.95

Gibraltar Directory 1883   Gibreprint No.1
   by Major George J Gilbard
Facsimile reprint with an introduction by Tito Benady.
ISBN 0 948466 26 X   £20.00

The Mating Cry of the Dodo
   by Giannito
Satirical essays on the political situation in Gibraltar in 1977.
Paperback
ISBN 0 948466 02 2   £1.50

Gibguides

Handy pocket-guides to Gibraltar, lavishly illustrated with colour photographs.

No.1 Gibraltar Guidebook
  by Tito Benady 3rd edition
ISBN 0 948466 13 8   £2.95

No.2 The Flowers and Wildlife of Gibraltar
  by John Cortés and Clive Finlayson
ISBN 0 948466 07 3   £2.95

No.3 Guide to the Gibraltar Museum
  by Tito Benady
ISBN 0 948466 10 3   £2.25

Translations of Gibguide No.1
  Gula de Gibraltar *Spanish* ISBN 0 948466 17 0   £2.95
  Guide de Gibraltar *French* ISBN 0 948466 18 9   £2.95
  Reisefuhrer von Gibraltar *German* ISBN 0 948466 19 7   £2.95

Due in October 1992

The Royal Navy at Gibraltar by Tito Benady
Gibraltar's naval history from the 16th. century to our own day with four chapters on World War II. With over 90 black and white illustrations. Published in conjunction with Maritime Books.
Casebound
ISBN 0 907771 49 1   *£25 estimated*

Angling in the Strait of Gibraltar by Hubert Caetano
A pocket guide to the fish and fishing in the area, extensively illustrated.
Original paperback
ISBN 0 948466 25 1   *£9 estimated*

The Streets of Gibraltar
A historical guide to the town of Gibraltar, its streets and ancient buildings, with drawings by George Felipes.
ISBN 0 948466 27 8   *In preparation*

As he approached the counter, he reached into his pocket.

Withdrawing his hand, he pushed his way through a group of men. Silence spread across the room, as he faced Julio.

'Yours, I think.'

Amongst the group by the bar, all eyes turned to the large stone (not the same one, but Julio would never know that), the crumpled paper, and the string he deposited in a pool of spilt beer.

He picked up the heavy brass knocker on the solid oak door and banged hard, perhaps too hard.

The door opened. Rosana stood before him. Her eyes widened.

'What are *you* doing here?'

'I had to come back to Spain, to complete an investigation.'

'Was that the only reason?'

'Why else would I come?'

Her expression grew in intensity. She took a deep breath as her elbows rose in unison, and she planted her hands on her hips.

'Miguel-Ángel Fernand...' was all she could say before he kissed her.